A PICTORIAL HISTORY OF HIGHWAY 99
The Scenic Route

A Pictorial History of

HIGHWAY 99

The Scenic Route

REDDING, CALIFORNIA TO PORTLAND, OREGON

Carole MacRobert Steele

LUMINARE PRESS

WWW.LUMINAREPRESS.COM

A Pictorial History of Highway 99: The Scenic Route
Copyright © 2021 by Carole MacRobert Steele

Printed in the United States of America

Cover Design by Claire Flint Last

Luminare Press
442 Charnelton St.
Eugene, OR 97401
www.luminarepress.com

LCCN: 2020923172
ISBN: 978-1-64388-436-3

This book is dedicated to my husband, who has lovingly supported my enthusiasm for the old highway and the writing of this book. Over the past fifty years Frank and I have traveled up and down "Old 99" in California and Oregon. In recent years we've searched out the abandoned and less traveled sections of the highway.

I'd also like to acknowledge Jill Livingston (Living Gold Press) for publishing the excellent That Ribbon of Highway *book series where she gives detailed history, instructions, and maps for traveling Old Highway 99 in California and Oregon. Without her books, we wouldn't have been able to locate some of the highway sections. I have great respect for the effort and dedication it took on her part to research, photograph, and write the history of Highway 99.*

TABLE OF CONTENTS

CALIFORNIA

OREGON

INTRODUCTION

⸻⸺⸺

Readers often wonder why a person chooses to write about a particular subject. For me, it was nostalgia ... a yearning for times gone by and an appreciation of a more simplistic and gentler era.

Personal memories as a child traveling on "Old 99" in the 1950's and 1960's led me to write this book. I wanted to share with people having similar interests in travel history my collection of 600+ vintage Highway 99 postcards.

For over forty years I've been collecting and selling old postcards. One of my areas of interest included old Highway 99. Years ago I started amassing as many Highway 99 postcards as I could find; focusing mainly on the road itself and gradually including main streets, gas stations, restaurants, motels, and roadside attractions.

My goal is to preserve these scenes in a pictorial book capturing the Golden Age of the Pacific Highway/Highway 99 from the mid-1920's to the 1960's. Although still a scenic drive, Interstate 5 through California and Oregon bypasses all the towns; thus losing the charm of road travel as it was in olden days.

It wasn't realistic to try and acquire a postcard view of every town, gas station, motel, or cafe along the route from California through Oregon. What I strive to do in this book is to show representative views through the decades while achieving a sense of what life was like along the highway. Rather than burden the reader with a lot of detailed text, I instead captioned each photo with noteworthy facts and light history. For a more extensive history of Old 99, several books have been written on the subject as listed in the Bibliography at the back of the book.

Highway 99 stretched from the U.S. border of Mexico north to the border of Canada, but I chose to cover only the most scenic miles from Red Bluff, California to Portland, Oregon. My childhood memories originate back while traveling this section of the highway every summer from our home in the San Francisco Bay Area to visit relatives in Portland.

Mom, Dad, sister, and I loaded into our 1955 Mercury station wagon and started the thirteen hour drive to Portland along Old 99. It was Dad's responsibility to prepare the car for the trip, load the suitcases, and do all the driving. He made sure we had the canvas water bag to hang on the front bumper in case the radiator overheated going up steep grades through the mountains. Mom's responsibility was to pack the suitcases and prepare food for lunch and snacks. As the one not doing the driving, Mom also had to try and keep the peace between my sister and I as we often bickered during the strain of the long ride.

The "Old Merc" had no air conditioning or power steering. It was miserable trying to bear the extreme heat of Red Bluff and Redding where summer temperatures could reach well over one hundred degrees. My sister and I whiled away the hours counting billboards, reading, or coloring. As kids often do, we annoyed our parents by constantly asking, "Are we there yet?" We never stopped overnight in a motel, nor did we stop at A&W for a hamburger or root beer. Mom packed tuna or egg sandwiches and a thermos of milk. We stopped for gas at various towns along the way with Dad asking the uniformed attendant to "fill 'er up." In those days, it was a common practice for the attendant to "check under the hood" for oil levels, radiator water level, and clean the windshield.

In the 1950's, certain stretches of the two lane road were narrow, twisty, and steep. When Dad got behind a truck he couldn't pass, he'd get very impatient and honk his horn at the poor driver. He'd curse saying, "Those damned Oregon drivers!"

Exhausted from the long trip, we were happy and excited to finally arrive at Grandma and Grandpa's house in Portland. By the mid-1960's we were driving to Portland in a big Oldsmobile with all its amenities. It now only took ten hours on the newly-completed Interstate 5. I was eighteen in 1966 when we took our last trip together as a family; my sister was twenty.

Trying to think back sixty years, I wish my memories were more vivid and detailed of the towns we drove through, or of the highway itself. One lasting memory I still have as I drive I-5 today is that of Black Butte and Mt. Shasta in California. Through a child's eyes, their "bigness" awed and inspired me. Black Butte, with its intriguing black volcanic coloring and lack of trees, rises abruptly from the ground along Old 99. My postcards depict how the road literally ran along the base of the mountain.

Before you start this pictorial journey, I want you to have a clear picture of what road travel was like in the early decades. The photographs will be more meaningful if you understand the history of lodging, gas stations, eateries, and tourist attractions.

All the photos in this book are shown in the condition in which they were purchased with any stains, creases, tears, over-exposure, or under-exposure.

Enjoy the Ride!

Carole MacRobert Steele

Auto Travel on the Pacific Highway and Old 99

1910–1960's

⸺⟨⟩⸺

Henry Ford's "Tin Lizzie" Model T, built from 1908 to 1927, was the car that put America on wheels. It was popular because it was durable, versatile, and easily maintained. Henry Ford once said, "You can have any color … as long as it's black." Because Model T's were mass-produced, they were affordable for most everyone. Even with dirt and mud roads, Americans wanted to travel and see sights outside their own environs.

Model T's could seat eight people. For lack of windows, clear isinglass was used that could be rolled up and down to protect passengers from the elements. Top speed was twenty-five miles per hour which equaled about one hundred miles in thirteen hours. Traveling thirty-five to forty-five miles was considered a "big trip." No wonder auto tent camping soon became popular; since there was no lodging available along rural roadways.

Not only was lodging scarce, but so was gas, food, and restrooms. Travelers resorted to hiding in the brush to go to the bathroom. To bathe, they brought along a wash pan, bar of soap, and a jug of water. Dinner might consist of weenies and onions, or potatoes and kraut cooked over a campfire. Running out of gas meant having to flag down another motorist to siphon gas from his gas can strapped on the running board.

A flat tire every thirty-five miles was considered normal. Repairs were done by lantern light; or the driver could opt to bump home on the tire rim. Getting through mud was the most challenging. If stuck, the car was put in low gear and full-throttled to plow through the mud. If that didn't work, a friendly farmer might be willing to use his mule team to pull you out. And if that wasn't enough, thieves might steal your batteries and tires if the car was left unattended; valuable commodities in those days. The Model T was equipped with three foot pedals:

forward, reverse, and brake. The accelerator lever was under the steering wheel and was operated by using the right hand. From 1927 to 1931 Ford produced the Model A with many improvements over the Model T; making travel easier with more comfort and reliability.

Motorists were appreciative of the State Highway Commissions when they built roadside drinking fountains in the 1930's. Signs read: Good Drinking Water 300' Ahead. Each fountain was designed to harmonize with the particular scenic countryside where it was located. At a cost of two to three hundred dollars each, they were built by highway maintenance workers using masonry rubble. A pipe projected out of the fountain and each fountain had a buffer for drinking. A little pool was used to fill radiators or to let pets drink. The water was tested for potability. To keep from freezing in the winter, the shut-off valve was turned off.

The story of the Pacific Highway and Old Highway 99 starts in 1910 when California, Oregon, and Washington agreed there was a need for one road connecting the three States. This road became known as the Pacific Highway ... not to be confused with the Pacific Coast Highway. It followed the old stagecoach trail from the Mexican border to the Canadian border, and was often called the "Highway of Three Nations."

People who lived in towns and cities were anxious to experience the "eye-dazzling views of forested mountains, lush valleys, swift-flowing rivers, and picturesque towns that awaited around every sweeping curve" ... describing precisely the most scenic part of the Pacific Highway and Highway 99 between Redding and Portland.

Following the contours of the land using shovels, wheelbarrows, and horse-drawn scrapers, construction of the highway began in California in 1914. The road surface consisted of crushed rock sixteen feet wide; suitable for fifty to one hundred cars to travel in a day. Although better than the earlier dirt road, it was still rough, dusty, crooked, narrow, and steep. Drivers had to be either courageous or foolish to drive the mountain roads of Northern California and Southern Oregon.

The cry for "Get Oregon Out of the Mud" was heard loud and clear in 1913 when the Legislature created the Oregon State Highway Department. Up until then there was only twenty-five miles of paved road in the entire State! By 1914 the System had developed a route running north and south that was to be called the Pacific Highway. The first construction began in the city of Medford in southern Oregon.

The Siskiyou's were once described as, "an abrupt rugged chain of mountains, grand and imposing, covered with dense forests and deep canyons." This portion of road from Ashland, Oregon over the Siskiyou's to the California State border was completed in 1915. Although wide and gently graded, it was still just a dirt road; but now for the first time, thousands of people from all over the nation could enter Oregon from California driving an automobile. Medford began to heavily promote tourism to take advantage of this increase in human traffic.

In 1916, under the new California Division of Highways, modernization and improvements began on the Pacific Highway from Redding to the Oregon border. By 1920, the Pacific Highway, with its newly paved surface, afforded year-round access for travelers. In 1922 Oregon claimed it was, "The first State west of the Mississippi to have a paved highway the entire length of the State from the Columbia River to the California State line."

With an increased interest in traveling, there was still much to do as motorists began demanding even greater road improvements. Because of increased traffic speed, safety and comfort became top issues. Soon plans were being made to eliminate as many steep grades and sharp curves as possible with new and improved road alignments. Many bridges would need to be built and the pavement expanded to wider widths. Mileage and directional signs needed to be erected along the roadside. In 1925, U. S. Highway 99 shields appeared. The white shields with black lettering measured eighteen by eighteen inches and were made of sixteen gauge embossed steel enamel. By 1926, the Highway ran fifteen hundred miles from San Diego to Vancouver, but still needed continued upgrading. In 1928, U.S. Highway 99 was declared the longest improved highway in the United States … quite an accomplishment!

In the early 1940's, the Pacific Highway, now known as Highway 99, was recognized as "The Gateway to the Northwest." Gas stations, garages, auto camps, and motels were rapidly being built to accommodate the traffic. With this increased use, the Highway was once again improved by widening it to four lanes. In 1943 this improvement cost $35 million dollars.

There were now so many automobiles on the road, that by the mid-1950's, a Federal Highway Act was legislated requiring a thirteen year nationwide program that included a "national system of interstate and defense highways." Interstate 5, or I-5, as it's more commonly called, was built to run the entire length of California, Oregon, and Washington. It was constructed as a four-lane "super" highway resulting in the partial elimination of Old 99 as the main route of travel. The "Mom and Pop" roadside culture of gas stations, cafes, and motels began to die as travelers stayed on the big new Interstate to get to their destination.

After a decade of construction, using hundreds of men and tons of equipment, Interstate 5 was officially completed on October 22, 1966. In the last sixty years, for anyone who has traveled on I-5, knows it's constantly being worked on … widened, realigned, repaved, or new bridges built.

In 1993, California Assemblymen (former TV news anchor) Stan Statham, introduced a resolution to recognize U.S. 99 as part of California's heritage. Resolution AJR19 required CALTRANS (California Department of Transportation) to identify any remaining portions as "Historic Highway 99" … proclaiming: "U. S. 99 Highway system was instrumental in moving people and expanding business throughout the State." The Resolution passed on September 3, 1992, and HISTORIC 99 road shields were installed on former sections of the Route without using State funding.

Gas Stations—Fill 'Er Up

───⟨∞∞⟩───

In 1908 Model T's needed gasoline, and the common catch phrase became "fill 'er up." It was a cumbersome and time-consuming job for the attendant to get gas into the tank. Gas was often stored behind the grocery store and delivered to the motorist using a five gallon bucket and a funnel. In 1909 the first hand-operated pump came into use with the motorist being assured of getting the right amount of gas as indicated by a clock dial on the pump. Using a vertical brass tube, the manually operated piston pump measured one or five gallons into the tank.

In 1913 the world's first drive-up gas station opened. Cars pulled up to a brick and stucco service building using a concrete driveway. A canopy overhead protected the attendant and driver from the weather, and electricity lit up the station for night service. Many of these early stations were ugly little buildings, but by the mid-teens their appearance improved as a way to promote brand identity. Evolving from "service stations" to "filling stations," the best locations were on the main routes leaving town; near schools or at railroad crossings.

In 1914 California was to first State to offer free road maps to travelers, and by the 1920's, most States offered maps. Also during this time it was common to see attendants wearing uniforms. A "fill up" included having the windshield cleaned, tire pressures checked, and water and oil levels checked.

The 1920's saw changes and improvement in gas stations. In the beginning, only one grade of gasoline was available, but starting in 1925, "premium" grade was offered. Filling stations outnumbered the eighteen thousand garages that had sold gas. In 1920 there were now eight million cars on the road. By 1929 there were seventy-three millions cars with 143,000 drive-in stations to service them. Because there was a lot of competition, gas stations started building larger facilities and adding attractive landscaping. Islands offered several pumps to cut down on wait time. Wider driveways offered easier accessibility, and overhead canopies provided protection from the weather. Women especially favored … and demanded … immaculately clean restrooms.

In the 1930's gas stations expanded their service by adding cabins for lodging and a cafe for food. It was an all-in-one package that served everyone well, but attendants worked long hard hours and were paid low wages. They were expected to be knowledgeable about gas tank locations on various models of cars. They had to know how to check oil and water levels, take tire pressures, and do small repairs; while being courteous, friendly, and helpful … "service with a smile."

In 1940 there were 231,000 gas stations nationwide, but World War 11 brought construction of stations to a halt. With a lot men off to war, women had to take over pumping the gas. This was a small task compared to the thousands of women who were building war planes in factories!

The 1950's and 1960's saw gas stations stripped down and more functional. This was also the beginning of highway beautification efforts and the building of new interstates. Traveling motorists now had to exit the highway for gas; no more driving through little towns and hamlets to quickly pull into the corner gas station for a fill up.

Lodging—From Auto Tents To Motels

─⚬⚬⚬─

You have the car, you have the gas … now all you need is food and lodging. Auto gypsies, tin can tourists, squatters, gasoline bums, transients … all rather derogatory terms used to describe early automobile travelers. A nicer description for these adventurers would have been to call them "seasonal tourists." The poem written below by Ruth Raymond in the 1920's describes life in a tourist camp.

"A TIN CAN TOURIST CAMP"

'Neath spreading oak and pine tree tall "A tin can tourist"
in the Fall puts up his tent and plans to stay.

And soon another tourist comes.
They meet and greet like old time chums.

They tell new jokes and make new plans.
And mess from out the same tin cans.

Then other tourists come along.
The camp force now is growing strong.

Cars from the North, the East, the West bring weary tourists
seeking rest. All happy in the flowery glade beneath
the broad oaks welcome shade. They're singing songs and
making plans and piling up the empty cans.

And ere the blooming May comes around
they'll buy a piece of fertile ground.

And work it off in streets and squares. And every tourist
take some share for they will build a city there.

When they come back another year. Just as the tin can
tourist plans when he piles up the empty cans.

***

WITH THE ADVENT OF THE AUTOMOBILE IN THE DECADE OF 1910–1920, FAMILIES
yearned to hit the roads ... such as they were ... and see the country. They
shunned the idea of expensive hotel rooms; devising instead an inexpensive
alternative way. When evening neared, these travelers sought out secluded fields
or a grove of trees; sometimes on private property. They set up housekeeping for a
single night or a few days by gathering stones for a campfire, twigs and branches
for firewood, and toting water from a nearby stream or lake.

The "auto tent" was the mother of invention; a collapsible tent stored on,
and tied to, the running board of the car. The "rumble seat" in back held the
pillows, bedrolls, and cots. The tent folded out from the side of the car into a
full size shelter, but it offered no protection from the outdoor elements such as
mosquitoes, ants, poison ivy, ticks, snakes, or, other critters. The rear seat held
the stove, kerosene lantern, tarps, ropes, and luggage. It's amazing there was
any room left for people!

It wasn't long before NO CAMPING signs began popping up along the
road as property owners began to complain about people "squatting" on their
land without permission. Landowners put up barbed wire while the family dog
provided guard duty to scare away campers. Homeowners had every right to be
upset that their land was being trampled, defiled, and destroyed. Squatters left
campfires smoldering and trails of filth attracting flies. Orchards were picked
clean, chickens stolen, and cows milked dry.

Not all landowners resented the travelers. There were now so many cars on
the road that a profit could be made by renting out rooms in their homes. These
became known as "tourist homes" and were prevalent during the lean Depression years as a way of bringing in extra money.

In Oregon, the State Motor Association offered some auto camping Do's
and Dont's:

Slow down on curves and keep to the right

Roll bedding in a waterproof tarp

Bring no perishable food

A minimum of clothing, auto robe, and field glasses (binoculars)

Carry travelers checks; not cash or jewelry

Monitor gas and oil levels

Gather reliable information to avoid bad roads and detours

Travelers had a great fear of breaking down; so these rules were welcome advice.

With the rise of squatters, cities and towns recognized a need for organized camping, and by 1927 municipal auto camps began setting up clean campsites. There were now fifteen million motorists on the road. Economically speaking, townships realized that local businesses could benefit by offering free campsites to all who stopped. Although located on remote acres on the outskirts of the town, travelers still needed supplies and services. It was a win-win situation for all.

Municipal camps offered amenities that tent camping never did. Travelers were now offered the luxury of water fountains, picnic tables, showers, laundry facilities, electricity, and indoor flush toilets. These camps were so appealing they soon became overcrowded by attracting bums, hobos, and transients who overstayed their welcome while enjoying an unencumbered way of life. They ruined camp life for upper and middle class people who shied away; preferring instead to stay in privately owned camps. With this realization, the municipals began charging an overnight fee from fifty cents to $1.50, and limiting the length of stay. This would discourage the "undesirables" from hanging around.

By the early 1930's the camping experience evolved into auto cabin camps; rows of tiny salt box-shaped modest bungalows built along the road. Between 1929 and 1933, thousands of these little shacks were erected nationwide. Anyone with a minimal amount of money could get in on the boom. Mom and Pop owners could purchase a prefabricated cabin kit for $300 from the local lumberyard and expect to earn a yearly rental income of $2,800.

These crudely-made cabins were basically a square box with asphalt shingles with one door, no electricity, no indoor plumbing, two windows with no curtains, no insulation, open rafters, and bare floors and walls. Cooking was done outside over a campfire. There was a pot belly stove for warmth in the winter and oil lanterns or candles were used for lighting. Furnishings were sparse and included a wood bed frame with taut ropes and a bedroll. Travelers had to bring their own bedding and linens. There was only a table for two and a couple of chairs.

The cabin proprietors always lived on the premises. Their home was used as the Camp Office where they collected cabin fees. Cabins that had a mattress cost one dollar; blankets and sheets were an extra fifty cents. The Camp manager often rode on the running board of the car to show the renters the way to their cabin. A bucket of water from the hydrant was offered; as well as an armload of firewood. Because of their flimsy construction, the cabins deteriorated quickly.

Gas stations and diners were the first to jump on the lodging bandwagon by eliminating the need for travelers to drive to town for gas and food. By the mid-1930's, fourteen hundred gas stations had added auto camps or diners to their property. The gas station owner's family members helped with the duties. Dad managed the cars and gas while Mom served as hostess, cooked the meals, and did the laundry. Brother swept up and loaded the soda machine while sister cleaned the cabins.

Deluxe cabins had a sink, toilet, shower, stove, bed, dresser, and chair. Travelers in the 1930's were getting spoiled by demanding better accommodations. These better cabins were referred to as "cottage courts" built around a lush lawn or court. Operators were known as "courters." The main attraction was privacy; unlike camping with noisy neighbors and campfire smoke. Prices rose from seventy-five cents a night to $3.50 for a deluxe unit. Extra bedding and linens cost twenty-five cents. For this increased nightly charge, renters got a private bathroom, kitchenette with pots and pans, rugs, dressing table, bureau, radio, steam heat, and an attached garage. Travelers had it so good they could comfortably stay for a week or longer. Maps, newspapers, and tourist guides advertised these inexpensive convenient courts while hotel owners grew angry because their business was being stolen away. Most camps, cabins, and courts gave away free postcards as an advertising gimmick; and without those postcards, I couldn't have written this book!

In the 1930's motels offered greater comfort and convenience. The term MOTEL was first used in Arthur Heineman's Milestone Motel in San Luis Obispo, California; a contraction of MOTOR and HOTEL.

In the 1940's, Mom and Pop had to choose between economy or ambiance when selecting a location to build their motel; since location was the most important factor. Climate was imperative for year-round operation, as well as easy on/off highway access, beautiful natural surroundings, sufficient space for parking, and proximity to the nearest town. With their day starting at six in the morning, Mom and Pop never got away from the motel, and they only earned a modest income if their motel had less than twenty units.

Ideally, a typical motel room in the 1950's had to be at least fourteen feet by fourteen feet, have a vanity, bureau with two drawers, wall-to-wall carpet, tile bath, a bed with no foot boards, baggage stand, and a writing desk. The room colors were preferably warm and homey. Air conditioning, thermostat heating, and television were a must.

The American motel had become a true "home away from home" by the late 1950's, but popularity declined as they tried to compete with the big chain motels. It was too expensive for the upkeep required, utilities, remodeling, and the "freebies" that guests expected. The new interstate highways were beginning to bypass these small roadside motels. Higher quality motels were able to continue in business if they made a good first impression with attractive landscaping, pool, cafe, phones, and tv's in the room. Some owners resorted to using clever names or elaborate neon signs to attract travelers.

As the 1960's approached, the word "motel" became outdated, and terms like hotel, lodge, or suite were now being used. MOTEL 6 has remained successful and is still in business today … but not for $6.00 a night!

Most of the early roadside lodging has been torn down, crumbled, decayed, or disappeared into the overgrowth. Decades-old small motels are no longer desirable and modern, but they're still renting rooms; often to transients who rent weekly or monthly. Drive along any road in any State and you're likely to see several abandoned motels that are falling down; windows broken out and graffiti sprayed on the walls. Nostalgic depictions on vintage postcards are all we have left to remember the fabulous roadside lodgings of yesteryear.

Real Photo Postcards
and Photographers

The majority of postcards shown in this book are what is known in the hobby of postcard collecting as REAL PHOTOS. Simply put, they are actual black and white photographs printed on card stock paper with the words POST CARD on the back; along with a stamp box for postage. Postcard collectors consider these some of the most valuable and highly sought. Depending on subject matter, they can sell for hundreds of dollars each.

Real photo postcards captured American life at the turn of the century well into the 1940's when color Kodachrome postcards became popular. Postcards documented towns, historical events, disasters, occupations, businesses etc. In 1906, at the height of postcard popularity, Kodak introduced a camera that ordinary people could use to take pictures of their daily life. By sending their film to Kodak for developing, Kodak could print the photos on POST CARD back paper suitable for mailing. This practice became the rage as friends and family could now send each other a photo postcard of the new plow horse, the new baby, the new house, or Aunt Pittypat's new hat!

Meanwhile, professional photographers were busy traveling the countryside capturing hometown images to sell in their studio. The studio was often a rented building or their own home. It consisted of a lobby to greet customers and complete business transactions, and a separate room for postcard printing production.

Photographers took out ads in the local newspaper to market their photo postcards. They peddled their cards at tourist attractions, fairs, and community events. Some resorted to setting up a stand on the street corner as a way to sell cards. If there was a natural disaster or human tragedy, an opportunity was not missed to record it on a photo postcard to sell at a later date. Train wrecks and storm damage were popular subjects.

Expanding their photo business often involved enlisting the help of friends and family to handle the developing, printing, and delivery of wholesale lots of postcards. They considered themselves a postcard company as they reached out to local businesses to purchase bulk quantities of cards; who in turn, sold them to townspeople or tourists. Businesses who purchased postcards included pharmacies, general stores, hotels, resorts, and cafes etc.

Cards were displayed in highly visible places; often in the front window of the store with a sign that read POST CARDS FOR SALE. Cards were kept in piles in store display cases, or in albums for customers to thumb through. In 1908, revolving spin racks were invented. If you frequent antique stores, you'll often see old postcards displayed in these type of racks; both floor and counter top models.

To be successful, the photographer needed several merchants to carry his postcards. This meant expanding his selling territory within a fifty mile radius of his home town; often going door-to-door carrying samples of his cards. Cards could either be purchased outright or reordered and delivered through the mail using a consignment agreement. Photographers were free to sell their cards wherever they wanted, but they tried to avoid towns where there was already an established photography business.

In the early 1900's, these traveling photographers used horse-drawn carriages or the railroad to get from town to town. When the Model T arrived in 1910, it provided a more comfortable and affordable method of travel. They were proud of their cars and often included them in them in the photo shot. Adaptations to the car were needed to carry all their tools of trade. Bumper straps had to be added to hold the camera equipment, and large boxes were mounted on the back; sometimes with the company name printed on the sides.

A favorite time for photographers to hit the road was June through September. Winter travel was avoided unless there was an unusually heavy snowfall or winter event that required capturing it for posterity. With the trees bare of leaves, the Fall season provided a particularly good opportunity for unobstructed views for picture taking.

Hazards of road travel in those early days are discussed in another section of this book, but looking at certain postcard views, you can see where more prolific and imaginative photographers hiked to the top of a hill to get just the right shot, or scramble down a ravine to get a river view.

Vagabond photographers were common. Away from home for weeks at a time, they traveled in wagons rigged for crude living accommodations. While taking orders along the way, the photographer could set up a tent as a roadside studio/office or makeshift darkroom. Some sent their glass plates and film back home for friends and family to process and fill orders.

This was the lowest level of production as it had to all be done by hand. By 1910, the first high-volume printing machine became available and regional producers and huge urban companies jumped on board, turning out a million cards a day. Some photographers sent in large quantities of their negatives to be printed.

Some aspects of production were still labor intensive; such as developing negatives by hand and captioning. The most common caption was written by hand on the negative using India ink. The photographer was most often the one doing the captioning using his own distinct writing style and signature.

Real Photo postcards sold in stores for two to five cents each. The studio photographer also retailed them at that price. By today's prices, that equals fifty cents to one dollar each. By 1930, real photo postcards were still selling for five cents each. Postcards had to be printed on special paper and purchased in large volume. Other business costs included developing chemicals, film, wages, and rent.

Thanks to the real photo postcard, highways, cafes, gas stations, hotels, auto courts, motels, and roadside attractions have been captured on film for current and future generations to appreciate and study.

Some of the prolific photographers appearing in this book include:

DOT DOTSON. In 1931 he opened a store and photo lab in Eugene, Oregon. He was a pioneer in the photo finishing industry and one of the first to process color film. Dotson Photography is still in business at 1668 Willamette Street, Eugene, Oregon.

Ralph J. EDDY was best known for Oregon postcards he created and sold in the 1920's-40's. Ralph, and his brother Watson, started out by opening a studio in Portland, Oregon; but moving to nearby Oregon City in 1915 where they specialized in postcards of Oregon. In the summer months of the 1930's, Ralph and his wife Lillie, operated a stand selling their postcards at "Eddie's Place" along the Columbia River. Ralph died in 1970.

Frank "PAT" PATTERSON was the most well-known and prolific of all the California and Oregon photographers during the 1920's and 30's. Tourists and travelers purchased his postcards depicting natural landscapes, tourist sites, and highways in Oregon and northern California. The clarity and quality of his images stand out above all others. He truly had an "eye" for composing the best elements of the scene he was shooting. His real photo postcards are highly prized, costly, and greatly sought after by collectors.

Patterson was born in Washington in 1883. He married Cora in 1907 and they had three daughters. After they divorced in 1921, Frank moved to Medford, Oregon where he opened a photography studio. In

1922 he married Josephine and they moved to Santa Rosa, California in 1928. For reasons unknown to this writer, in the 1940's he spent six years in San Quentin prison. Upon release, he worked for Bear Photo in San Francisco until 1959. About this time, he developed Alzheimer's and was admitted to the Napa State Hospital in Napa, California where he died in 1961.

California

CHAPTER I

Red Bluff to Shasta Lake

Red Bluff

The city of Red Bluff is located in Tehama County on the West bank of the Sacramento River, and sits at the junction of US 99 and State Highway 36. Named for the reddish-colored low sandy bluffs on which it stands, it's the gateway to Lassen National Park. In the early days it was the chief trading center for the upper Sacramento Valley. The original route of US 99 ran through its grazing lands.

Pacific Highway near Red Bluff. Two 1930's cars. Road is paved with white center line and railings.

Riverside Auto Camp "On the banks of the beautiful Sacramento River at Red Bluff at West end of Sacramento River Bridge. Every cabin with bath, lavatory, hot and cold water, gas, and locked garage. Hotel service day and night." Photos shows a single iron bed frame, shower, toilet with wooden seat, two chairs, table, curtain on window. Office is the main building in the center.

Riverside Auto Camp. Shows individual garages with sliding doors; a little landscaping at the front of each door and a screen on each door.

Carole MacRobert Steele

Redding

Old Highway 99 has been renumbered Route 273 through Redding and is known as Market Street.

Redding's population doubled during the 1930's when Shasta Dam was built. The city was founded in 1873, and by 1939 it had a population of 4,188. The seat of Shasta County, the City lies at the head of the Sacramento Valley and was named after B. B. Redding, a Central Pacific Railroad land agent. The City was a shipping point for fruit, farming, and mining.

Before World War II, the approach to town on Highway 99 was known as the Miracle Mile because of the growth in gas, food, and lodging accommodating increased road travel.

English Villa Motel, 3010 Market Street (US Highway 99 S). 1950's era. Owners, Captain and Mrs. L. E. Hawkins. 12 units with kitchenettes, garage, shade trees, lawn chairs. Telephone 975.

Market St. - Redding, aka Miracle Mile; formerly US Route 99. Hotel Redding on the left. Cascade Theatre on the right. 25 mph sign on curb corner.

Grande Cafe, 1084 Market St. 1940's. Phone 547. (now Hinkle's Market and Sporting Goods). Located just before Market St. crosses the Sacramento River and becomes N. Market. Breakfast, lunch, dinner, fountain.

"On Hiway 99 entering Redding." Postmarked 1946 from Redding. This is the Miracle Mile aka N. Market St. Message on back: "Here is a picture of the highway leading into Redding. The mountains in the distance are covered with snow … you should see all the beautiful Christmas trees along the way." Road is two lanes paved with center white line.

1960's showing four lanes, river and bridge. "Miracle Mile" N. Market St. coming South from Yreka, or coming from downtown crossing the Sacramento River Bridge going North. Casa Blanca Motel on the left at 413 N. Market.

City Limit Auto Court. 1930's showing cabins with carports.

Motel 99. 1940's. 533 N. Market St./Highway 99/Miracle Mile. Air-cooled, landscaped, paved, awnings. Office is the main building on the right.

Monterey Court 1940's snapshot. 525 N. Market St. showing the Motel 99 next door! Air-cooled; open garages.

Monterey Court 1940's. 525 N. Market St. US 99. "fully modern 21 units; air conditioned, complete with tile showers and electricity; heat, radios, some kitchenettes." Office is center building. Phone 1106N

Hotel Casa Blanca 1/2 mile N. of Redding on US 99. 413 N. Market. Phone Redding 2360. "50 ultra-modern air conditioned units, each with private telephone; fully carpeted, Beauty Rest equipped. Breakfast, lunch, dinner, cocktails." Shell Gas shown on lower right. Hotel site now an empty lot.

Hotel Casa Blanca. Same caption as card above.

1950's Casa Blanca Hotel, 413 N. Market. "75 ultra modern units cooled by refrigeration, individual telephones, Beauty Rest mattresses, fully carpeted, swimming pool, coffee shop open 24 hours. Cashmere Room for dinning and dancing, cocktails." Phone Chestnut 1-4661

1970's Casa Blanca Motel, 413 N. Market. "Color cable TV, kitchenettes, queen size beds, king size water beds, doubles, large pool." (The restaurant as seen in previous views is now gone, as well as the trees with just a lawn area.)

FRANCISCAN COURT
REDDING, CALIFORNIA

Pre-1950 Franciscan Court. "1/2 mile N. of Redding, US Highway 99." Air conditioned, electric heat, member of United Motor Courts, open garages. N. Market Street. Lawn area with chairs and a lawn swing.

1930's Sacramento River Bridge at Redding, Pacific Highway (aka N. Market Street Bridge). In 1936 a new and wider bridge was built to accommodate Highway 99 traffic located a short distance to the East of the Dieselhorst Bridge.

Bridges at Redding, Calif. The bridge in the background is the Union Pacific truss over the Sacramento River built in 1939; one hundred ten feet above the River and 4,348 feet long ... aka Sacramento River Railroad Viaduct. The bridge in the foreground is the Market Street/Sacramento River Bridge.

Dieselhorst Bridge

The DIESELHORST BRIDGE, also known as Reid's Ferry Bridge, was built in 1915. In 1851, Reid's Ferry established a main crossing on the Sacramento River for the road from Shasta. The Reid's sold their ferry crossing to John and Charles Dieselhorst. The brothers constructed what was to be the first and oldest remaining concrete bridge on the Sacramento River. The Dieselhorst Bridge at six hundred thirty-nine feet long, is on the National Register of Historical Places. Closed to traffic in 1997, it had been in constant use until completion of the N. Court Street Bridge. It's now used strictly by pedestrians.

Highway Bridge at Redding, Ca. postmarked 1929. This is the Diselhorst Bridge showing the "old swimming hole" in the foreground; a gathering spot for young and old during hot Redding summers.

"A remarkable view of the Pacific Highway Bridge mirrored in the Sacramento River at Redding, Ca. "Old Swimming Hole" postmarked 1935.

Carole MacRobert Steele

Dieselhorst Auto Camp

Gotlieb Dieselhorst owned eighty-four acres on the South side of the Sacramento River. He purchased the land in 1859 for $2,500. The area was known as "Poverty Flat." After Gotlieb died in 1903, sons John and Charles, established an auto camp in the 1920's just west of the Dieselhorst Bridge. It was one of the first auto camps in Northern California. The Camp started out with a row of tent spaces. These spaces were constructed of wood with a roof. The cars parked beside the space. In the 1920's and 1930's, the brothers built thirty-one small cabins on the banks of the River. Because the summer population was exploding, they added a gas station and a store. John also built flat-bottom boats so people could go fishing and duck hunting. In the summer this location was the coolest place in Redding as people flocked to the nearby "swimming hole." The Dieslhorsts even hosted a water carnival. This thriving era all came to an end during the disastrous flood of 1940 when all the cabins and twelve acres washed away. In 1977 the last Dieselhorst descendant sold the land to the City to build a park. In 2009 a dozen remnants of concrete cabin pads were discovered laying beneath decades of overgrown blackberry bushes. In 2011, the E. Clampus Vitus Chapter 62 placed two plaques marking the site of Reid's Ferry and Dieselhorst Auto Camp.

"Cabins at Dieselhorst Auto Camp, Redding, Ca." 1930's. Each has a garage. It was located at Middle Creeks Rd. and Benton Dr.

"Riverside Auto Camp, Redding, Cal" (now N. Market St. coming from the South heading North). 1930's. "Store and Service Station." Mr. West, Prop. There's a big AUTO CAMP sign visible.

HIGHWAY BRIDGE, REDDING, CALIFORNIA . 7096

"Highway Br., Redding, Calif." Market Street Bridge entering Redding from the North to the South; 1940's. Two paved lane with white center line.

"Over Sacramento River at Redding, Ca." 1940s

"Eddy's Service and Camp - Eddy's Oasis." Homemade ice cream. Single gas pump. 5 Miles North of Redding. Possibly cabins on the right. 1930's.

River View Tavern, Hwy 99 near Redding. Postmarked 1949. Must have had a view of the Sacramento River from inside the tavern.

"At the Buffalo Ranch near Redding. 12 miles North of Redding at Mountain Gate near Bass Hill." "See the live buffalo." Patio chairs and snack bar with racks of post-cards visible. This Texaco Station had eight live buffalo located on Hwy 99 which went through Mountain Gate. When the construction of Interstate 5 wiped out the old Hwy 99 alignment, it resulted in the closure of the Texaco Station; as well as the motel, restaurant, and grocery store.

Carole MacRobert Steele

"Lakehead, Calif. A fine resort area noted for its fishing and hunting. Located on Hwy 99 near Dunsmuir." Twenty-five miles North of Redding, KLUB KLONDIKE is an old-fashioned roadhouse located on Main and Moody Streets. It's the oldest bar in Lakehead, and the building housed the town's first library and post office. It is rumored to have once had a brothel upstairs. Local history and rock 'n roll memorabilia cover the walls. There's a small stage for performances; shuffleboard, pool table, long bar, and chairs in front of the fireplace. Beer is cheap.

26 miles No. of Redding on U. S. 99, *Rambi Motel* LAKEHEAD, CALIF.

Rambi Motel, 1940's. Twenty-six miles North of Redding at Lakehead, Ca. Office on the right. Singles, doubles, and kitchens. Postmarked 1960. Phone Lakehead 1. "A new fully modern, air-cooled motel with showers and garages." Mr. and Mrs. Wenman, owners.

Lakeshore Resort, Calif. 1940's. This was the Lakeshore Inn and RV, oldest resort on Shasta Lake. It burned down in 1996. Located at 20483 Lakeshore Dr., Lakehead. Shows cabins. "Lakeshore Service" with 1940's car and three MOBIL gas pumps.

KLUB KLONDIKE "Noted for its friendly atmosphere, fine foods, and beverages. Known by tourists from Canada to Mexico." Located on Hwy 99 at Lakehead, Ca. near Shasta Lake. Coffee shop and dinners. 1960's.

Carole MacRobert Steele

Greetings from Redding, California. Postmarked 1941.

"On the Pacific Highway near Redding, Calif." 1940s.

"May 5, 1939 Redding, Calif." Young man by CALIFORNIA US 99 highway shield.

Carole MacRobert Steele

The Gables—Hwy 99. Thirty-three miles North of Redding. 1940s. A cafe and two UNION 76 gas pumps. Sign reads: "Blow horn for services. Hamburgers and can beer to go."

Sacramento River Canyon

SACRAMENTO RIVER CANYON lies North of Redding to Dunsmuir. The railroad was built through the Canyon in the 1880's and soon towns and resorts sprang up along its route. When the highway arrived, the road and railroad tracks had to safely co-exist. Slides were a problem, so craftsmen built retaining walls and more bridges were built. In the early 1930's you'd drive from Redding in the morning and arrive at Dunsmuir by night. Today we travel it in less than one hour.

ON HIGHWAY 99 NEAR REDDING, CALIF.
J.H. EASTMAN B-1394

1940's on Hwy 99 near Redding. View shows the two Riverview train trestles North of Lakehead on the East side of the freeway. The longer bridge is new; the smaller one is the original.

"Salt Creek Lodge" postmarked 1932 from Dunsmuir. Salt Creek Lodge Road, Lakehead. Message on back reads: "Salt Creek Lodge N. of Redding. Made 20 miles today. Had a bit of engine trouble and was delayed in Redding. Crossed Sacramento River 2 times." View shows entrance to the cabins, Salt Creek Garage and Automobile Repairing, Standard Oil products, and one gas pump; Highway in the foreground. Salt Creek Bridge crossed Salt Creek pre-1940's and wound its way along the creek. The road and bridge are now gone.

Pacific Highway Sacramento River. 1930's. Shows Dog Creek Bridge (aka Harlan D. Miller Bridge), and railroad tracks in the Sacramento River Canyon.

Sacramento River from Pacific Highway, postmarked 1937. Shows a Central Oregon and Pacific Railway concrete deck bridge over the River.

Carole MacRobert Steele

Dog Creek Bridge

DOG CREEK BRIDGE, built in an open arch style, was said to be one of the most artistic and spectacular structures ever built in California. It had four benches and pedestrian overlooks built into the roadway for weary travelers to rest and enjoy the scenery. The bridge crossed Dog Creek at its junction with the Sacramento River. Harlan Miller, one-time chief of the California Bridge Department, was involved in the bridge design, but he died before it was completed. The bridge was closed to traffic in 1974 when it was replaced by a newer bridge. Dog Creek Bridge was slated for demolition, but protestors and concerned local residents were successful in saving it. It's now protected under Federal law and became a California Historical Landmark on May 29, 1984.

1940's Dog Creek Bridge with rock arch railing. A little sign on the bridge says DOG CREEK. The road is paved with white center line.

1940's Pinehurst Motel near Mt. Shasta. Has a MOBIL Gas sign and one or two pumps; Highway in the foreground.

Pit River Bridge

Officially known as the Veteran's Of Foreign Wars Memorial Bridge, it crosses the Pit River arm of Shasta Lake. It was also known as the Bridge Bay Bridge and the Union Pacific/Pit River Bridge. In 1943, the "new" Pit River Bridge opened. It's a double-decker dual-purpose bridge with the Southern Pacific and Union Pacific Railroads using the lower level, while the upper level carries car traffic. Made of steel construction, it's 3,588' long and 70' wide. It was the tallest road-rail bridge in the world, and the highest rail bridge in the United States. When Shasta Dam was constructed, the Shasta Route of the Southern Pacific Railroad and US. Highway 99 were rerouted at a cost of $15,000,000.

Pit River Bridge over Shasta Lake 1940's. Shows land mass and the Lake still filling up.

Pit River Bridge. "World's highest double-deck highway and railroad structure." In this view the Lake is still filling up after completion.

Pit River Bridge. 1940's.

Carole MacRobert Steele

Auto and Rail Bridges over Shasta Lake. "These two modern bridges carry traffic over what was once a canyon of the Pit River. Now this canyon has become part of huge Shasta Lake formed by Shasta Dam." Visible in the background is the concrete bridge that has not yet been submerged, and there is a train on it!

A portion of Shasta Lake, postmarked 1953. Shows the land mass that would eventually be submerged to become what was then, and is now, the location of Bridge Bay Resort.

Shasta Reservoir—Pit River Bridge. The land mass in previous photo is now almost totally under water. The small sandy point is now Bridge Bay Resort showing a pier shelter with boats in the water.

Bridge Bay Resort located 12 miles North of Redding. Offers motel, dining, cocktails, marina, and houseboats. The Lake is now completely filled up.

Carole MacRobert Steele

1920s Sacramento River, Northern California. This is the original Pit River concrete bridge near its junction with the McCloud River. In 1914, because the new State highway followed the basic routing of the early toll road, many concrete bridges had to be built to cross the many streams in the mountains. The ferry was put out of business in 1916 when this arch bridge was completed. It had been the longest concrete span in the State. Just downstream, the "new" steel Pit River Bridge would be built. It would take several years for the old bridge to be completely submerged as Shasta Lake continued to fill.

Pacific Highway on McCloud River. The McCloud River parallels the Sacramento River fifteen miles North of Redding. The roadbed is visible on the right just above the river bed.

Pit River Pacific Highway. 1930's view of the original Pit River Bridge and Inn. This bridge now submerged under Shasta Lake. Pit River Inn sold food and sundries at the Southern approach to the concrete arch bridge built in 1916. The Inn was located at the Pit River crossing where the Pit joins the Sacramento River.

Pit River Bridge Inn, Pacific Highway, Ca. 1940s. The Inn and store were built in 1916 and are now all under Shasta Lake.

Pit River Bridge store. 1930's. Small sign at bridge entrance says: PIT RIVER. Nearby is a FOR SALE sign.

1940's Pit River Bridge with the old highway bridge in the foreground. Visible are the worker safety nets hanging from new bridge construction.

Pit River Bridge—highest double-deck span in the world. 500' from the river to the top deck; length 3590 feet. Arrow shows the old Highway 99 bridge; started in 1935 and finished in 1945. The Lake was full by 1948.

PIT RIVER BRIDGE" NEAR REDDING, CALIF.
J.H.EASTMAN B-1564

1940's Pit River Bridge being built showing workers, safety nets, and steel girders.

1940's Pit River Bridge 500' from the water to the top deck. Old original concrete bridge is in the background along the river bed.

Pit River Bridge on Highway 99 between Redding and Dunsmuir. Postmarked September, 1945. Message: "We have got to Redding. Car running like a top. Sure hot here."

Shasta Lake Auto and Rail Bridge. 1960's. "These 2 modern bridges carry traffic over what was once a canyon of Sacramento River. Now this canyon has become part of Shasta Lake." Railroad bridge in foreground and land now under water. Bridge across the water is the Antlers Bridge aka Sacramento River Bridge.

Paving the new highway bridge at Antler Creek; built 1941 and located at Lakehead/Lakeshore. California Department of Transportation demolished it in 2017 because it was inefficient in handling the increased flow of traffic. The new bridge was opened in 2018.

CHAPTER II

Shasta Dam and Shasta Lake

I n the years of the Depression, men came from all over the country to get a job building what was to become Shasta Dam and Lake. Forty-five hundred men were hired working twenty-four hours a day building this concrete arch gravity dam located at the junction of the Sacramento and Pit Rivers. It was called Kennett Dam before construction began; named after the old mining town that would be submerged when Shasta Lake began to fill.

Considered a great engineering feat, this was known as the "Central Valley Project." The Dam was needed for long-term water storage to irrigate the fertile agricultural land of California's Central Valley, and for flood control and hydro-electricity. Shasta Lake would be the largest reservoir in the State. The Dam and Lake were named after nearby snow-capped Mt. Shasta looming majestically in the distance. On January 2, 1945, the last of some fifteen million buckets of concrete was poured, making Shasta Dam the second highest dam in the world; surpassing Hoover Dam. Shasta Lake became the largest man-made lake and the third largest body of water in California. The project is owned by the U. S. Bureau of Reclamation.

Most of old Highway 99 disappeared when Shasta Lake began to fill up. Twenty-seven miles of railroad track and eighteen miles of highway had to be relocated. Even in the mid-1950's, ten years after the dam was completed, realignments and improvements were still needed.

General view of the SHASTA DAM site. Message written on back: "The Sacramento River looks small, but where the dam will be it was a 100' of water. They have to move 3,500,000 cubic yards of rock. Will take 6,000,000 cubic yards of concrete in the dam. The dam will be 560' high and 3500' long. Will back the water up 47 miles. They are going to move the two towns and there will be several hundred feet of water over them. The mess hall you see in the center seats 450 men at one time. The building to the right on the hill is the hospital having 75 beds. Also two large dormitories and 200 small houses."

Shasta Dam During Course of Construction

Shasta Dam during the course of construction. "The great Shasta Dam now under construction. When completed, it will be the second largest dam in the world. It will be 3500' long, 736' high, and contain 5,610,000 cubic yards of concrete; making it larger than the Great Pyramid in Egypt. It's reservoir will be capable of storing 4,500,000 acre feet of water."

Government City near Shasta Dam 1940's. Shows worker's small homes and neighborhoods.

Shasta Lake 1940's showing land mass not yet submerged. Dirt road and car visible.

Shasta Lake at the mouth of the Pit and McCloud Rivers, 1940's.

At Bridge Bay Resort on Shasta Lake mid-1950's. Sender's message: "Such is life. This is beautiful country. The lake is so pretty. Our cabin is so deluxe—twin beds too." Bridge Bay has the largest marina on the west coast with seven hundred slips. Located on Bridge Bay Road, it holds one hundred houseboats. Bridge visible in background.

Shasta Lake and Highway 99 visible on the right. 1950's.

The Three Shasta's: Shasta Dam, Shasta Lake and Mt. Shasta. 365 miles of shoreline. 1950's.

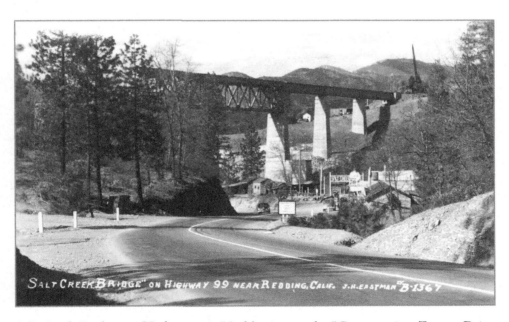

Salt Creek Bridge on Highway 99. Visible sign reads: "Construction Zone—Drive Carefully." 1940's Salt Creek store and Union 76 gas station.

Charlie Creek Bridge aka Lakeshore Drive Bridge. Dated on back 1925. Reinforced concrete arch bridge over Charlie Creek on Lakeshore Dr. at Lakehead; now under Shasta Lake. Harlan Miller, builder.

Carole MacRobert Steele

CHAPTER III

Shasta Lake to Dunsmuir

Mt. Shasta from Pacific Highway near Castella, California. 1920's dirt road.

Mt. Shasta from Pacific Highway, Sacramento Canyon. 1930's packed dirt road.

Pacific Highway near Redding. Stone arch wall.

Carole MacRobert Steele

Shasta from Sacramento Canyon near Sweetbriar. Shows railroad tracks and the tip of Castle Crags on the left. Road is oiled. Highway supported by masonry retaining wall. In this little valley there was once a small industry which produced hybrid strawberry plants known as "Sweetbriar".

Close-up of stone wall on Pacific Highway, 1930's. Sweetbriar shown down below with buildings and railroad tracks.

Castella

Located on the upper Sacramento River Canyon, Castella was originally called Castle Rock, but renamed Castella in the 1880's. The town survived by catering to vacationers coming to visit Castle Crags State Park and other attractions. Old Highway 99 ran through Castella and was called Main Street. Castle Rock Railway Station was built in the 1920's to serve vacationers coming to the area. Castella was also "the" place to visit during Prohibition. This out-of-the-way place was perfect for manufacturing liquor and, was the site of many illegal stills. Alcohol flowed freely with frequent raids on local saloons.

Mt. Shasta-Sweetbriar near Castella, 1940's. Rock arch wall and paved road with center white line.

Shasta from Highway 99; Sweetbriar/Castella, 1950's. This is the same view as book's cover photo.

Mt. Shasta from Sacramento Canyon, 1930's. Shasta River from Castella showing the town of Castella and the depot alongside the tracks.

Carole MacRobert Steele

Castella, California depot and saloon; pre-1920 showing a man with a horse and wagon. Forty-six miles North of Redding.

Cragview, Castella, Cal. Cabins at the resort; 1930's.

Highway 99 near Mt. Shasta, Calif. Shi-Lo Springs mineral baths, 1940's. Located on the Sacramento River at Sims Flat between Castella and Pollack; cabins, trailer camp, and store. The water is rich in sodium and lathers without soap. Three times daily the water changes color from clear, to yellow, to deep green.

Castle Crags

Castle Crags State Park, located in the Shasta Trinity National Forest, came into being as a result of the 1929 stock market crash. In 1933 the State acquired the land after private developers went bankrupt when their resort development failed. This Park contained fifty square miles of wilderness with jagged ridges of silver-gray granite reaching for the sky. In the 1930's, the boys of the Civilian Conservation Corps built its trails, roads, campsites, restrooms, and homes. Elevations range from 2000 feet along the Sacramento River to 6500 feet at their tallest summit. The Wintu Indians called the Crags the "Abode of the Devil." With campsites set among stately pines and streams and lakes stocked with fish, this is a popular place to vacation.

Castle Crags from Pacific Highway. 1930's dirt road.

Castle Crags from Pacific Highway, 1947. Road is now paved and has a white railing.

Carole MacRobert Steele

Castle Crags, California, 1940's

Castle Crags, 1940's. Car has California license plate. Road is crude dirt.

Carole MacRobert Steele

Castle Crags, 1940's. Joe Ammirati Meats, Grocery and Liquor; Chevron gas.

Castle Crags, 1940's. On the side of the building it reads: Ammirati's Meats, Groceries, Beer/Wine.

Castle Crags, 1960's. Still selling Chevron gas at Ammirati's grocery store; Interstate 5 in the foreground.

Ammirati's Market and Tavern, Castle Crags State Park, Castella. Still selling Chevron Gas, meats, groceries, liquor, and tavern. Ammirati's was established in 1929 as a grocery store and boarding house.

Carole MacRobert Steele

Real Log Cabins, Hot and Cold Water and Shower Baths, Castle Crags Farm, Shasta Co.
Property of PACIFIC IMPROVEMENT COMPANY, San Francisco.

Castle Crags Farm, Shasta Co., Property of Pacific Improvement Co., San Francisco. A 1913 travel guide states: "There is a trail up from the sheer wall of the mountains from Castle Crags Farm. Visible from the summit of Mt. Shasta, Mt. Lassen, Mt. Eddy, Black Butte, Eagle Peak."

Castle Crags Farm was situated where Soda Creek joins the Sacramento River. It was a leading summer resort. The Crags were reached by horseback on a trail.

Interior of Log Cabin with Shower Bath at Castle Crags Farm, Shasta County.
Property of PACIFIC IMPROVEMENT COMPANY, San Francisco.

Castle Crags Farm, Shasta Co., Property of Pacific Improvement Co., San Francisco. "Interior of log cabin with shower bath." Fireplace, dresser, bed, two chairs, table, carpeting, curtains.

CHAPTER IV

Dunsmuir to Weed

⨯

Dunsmuir

Perched on a narrow shelf along the winding canyon, Dunsmuir, California was founded in 1887 as a result of the completion of the Central Pacific Railroad. Known as the "Home of the Best Water on Earth", Alexander Dunsmuir donated a water fountain in 1888 to the new town, and the town was renamed in his honor. This fountain still remains functional. There are/were three fountains located on Dunsmuir Avenue. Shasta lava layers filter the drinking water so there is no need for additional filters. In the early years, Dunsmuir was called Poverty Flats, but by 1913, it was the largest community in Siskiyou County with a population of 2,700. Dunsmuir was the Shasta Division of the Southern Pacific Railroad. Still visible in the center of town are railroad shops and yards of the Southern Pacific. This Shasta Route ran the length of the Sacramento River Canyon, and the tracks are still in use today. By the 1950's, the town's population dropped. Southern Pacific changed from steam to diesel engines, and the payroll was down to five hundred workers. The roundhouse, shops, and company buildings were demolished . Dunsmuir has always been a favorite of fishermen and hunters, and recreation helps keep it thriving today.

The Weed Store

158 S Weed Blvd, Weed, CA
96094
(530) 938-4678

Main Outlet

Receipt #63359
12 Jun 2022 2:28pm

BOOK - A PICTORIAL
HISTORY OF HIGHWAY 99
 1 @ $24.99 $24.99

Subtotal $24.99
Total Tax (Tax, $1.87
7.5%)

TOTAL (1 items)   **$26.86**

Credit Card / Debit
Card $26.86
Sun, 12 Jun 22
2:28pm
EMV (VISA)
SIGNATURE NOT
REQUIRED
****0109   DEBIT
TRANS TYPE: PURCHASE
TRANS NO.:   819973271
Approval
Number: 078268
Host
Response   Approved
Message:
AID: A00000009808
                40
Application
Label: US DEBIT
                ARQC
Cryptogram: A500DAC811C7
                1A8A
ACCEPTED

TO PAY $0.00

---

www.Weedstore.com
FACEBOOK   @
WeedCalifornia

The Weed Store
158 S Weed Blvd, Weed, CA
96094
(530) 938-4618

Main Outlet

Receipt #63359
12 Jun 2022 2:28pm

BOOK - A PICTORIAL
HISTORY OF HIGHWAY 99
1 @ $24.99 $24.99

Subtotal $24.99
Total Tax (Tax) $1.87
(7.5%)

TOTAL (1 items) $26.86

Credit Card / Debit
Card $26.86
Sun, 12 Jun 22
2:28pm
EMV (VISA)
SIGNATURE NOT
REQUIRED
DEBIT   ****0109
PURCHASE   TRANS TYPE:
8189732/1   TRANS NO.:
             Approval
078268   Number:
             Host
Approved   Response
             Message:
A0000000098080   AID:
40
US DEBIT   Application
             Label:
ARQC
A50DAC8J1C7 Cryptogram:
2A8A
ACCEPTED

TO PAY $0.00

Highway 99 near Dunsmuir. 1940's paved road with white center line.

Mt. Shasta and Interstate 5. 1960's road sign says: Dunsmuir City Limit with the population and elevation.

Mt. Shasta from Pacific Highway. Road is paved and shows the future site of the Division of Motor Vehicles, State of California building.

Division of Motor Vehicles, State of California check station. This Division was established in 1915 for the registration of vehicles. A two dollar fee was charged, and the car owner was issued a circular shaped tag that had to be displayed on the vehicle. The License number had to be mounted on the rear showing three inch high black letters against a white background. Cars were inspected for satisfactory lamps, good brakes, and a bell or horn.

Carole MacRobert Steele

Mt. Shasta from Pacific Highway. The checking station shows a stopped car and truck. A STOP sign is on the side of the road indicating all cars must stop for inspection.

1930's Northern California Checking Station; Pacific Highway 99, Dunsmuir. Sign says: STOP—Out of State cars must STOP. Sign on building says: Division of Registration, Station No. 7, State of California. A booth sits nearby for TRAVEL INFORMATION and FREE MAPS for tourists.

1930's Highway 99, Dunsmuir, Calif. Written on the back: "This is a picture of the checking station for all out of State cars." Same as previous photo, but booth says SHELL TOURING SERVICE. In the early 1920's the California Department of Agriculture established Border Protection Stations to help keep fruit and vegetable pests coming into California from other States.

Railroad tracks at Dunsmuir 1930's-40's. The locomotive shelters seen on the right, still stand today.

Cottages at Brown's Auto Park 1930's. Reads: Brown's Auto Park with gas station pump in the background. Highway is paved with white center line.

Dunsmuir montage 1930's roadside billboard: "Dunsmuir Auto Court one mile N. of business district Hwy 99. Home Away From Home. It's the beds." Views show Mossbrae Brae Falls, fisherman in river, Mt. Shasta, fishing rod and reel, creel, net, and trout.

Shirley Camp N. of Dunsmuir, Pacific Highway 99 "Campers Row." In 1928 Dunsmuir had seven auto camps on Dunsmuir Avenue. Shirley's Camp was South of Cave Springs and is still there! This 1940's view shows the office building with clock time at noon. Sign reads: "Blow horn for manager." Stone drinking fountain and cabins visible to the left.

1940's SS Motel, Dunsmuir, Ca. Air conditioned and furnace heat. Sender's message: "The cabins on the other side to our home tonite."

Carole MacRobert Steele

1940's Oak-Lo Motel one mile N. of Dunsmuir; Phone 2198. Two new elegantly furnished 25 unit electrically heated motels with tubs and tile showers. Carpeted wall-to-wall. Heated and locked garages. Radios. Mr. and Mrs. J. Morgan Jones, owner/mgr. AAA recommended, Best Western Motels and Duncan Hines.

The Oak-Lo Motel in recent years had been a Best Western Choice Inn. As of 2008–2011, it was still getting Trip Adviser internet reviews and being rated POOR. The restaurant was still open twenty-four hours. In recent years, this motel has been abandoned. For decades it had been the jewel of I-5; an imposing structure on the highway hillside noticeable to all cars driving by. Last year my husband and I parked and walked around it. The windows have been busted out and the doors broken down; the inside trashed and vandalized with a lot of disturbing graffiti. A hurricane fence surrounds the and blackberry bushes have taken over the buildings. More recently, plywood boards now cover all the windows. It will eventually be torn down as a new motel has already been built nearby; but not on the same property.

1962 "Both new—one for quiet, one for view." Free TV, free coffee. "Hilltop" view of Mt. Shasta from every room. "Garden Units" for quiet with expansive lawns and garages.

Same caption as card above.

Same caption as card above dated 1957; interior guest room.

Early 1960's Oak-Lo Motel and House of Glass Restaurant and Lounge. Direct access from US 99 and I-5 at Dwight Way. East side of highway. Large heated pool, refrigerated air conditioning. Room phones, picture window view of Mt. Shasta.

Same caption as above, but different owner/manager. Now listed as Mr. and Mrs. Robt. L. Rogers.

Same caption as above, but now mentions color TV. View from House of Glass Restaurant on I-5.

Carole MacRobert Steele

Railroad Park, Dunsmuir with Castle Crags visible in the background. Since 1968, Bill and Delberta Murphy had collected, preserved, and renovated old railroad cars. The cars were transformed into lodging and rented to travelers and railroad buffs. Known also as the Caboose Motel, it offers cabins and an RV park. Located on Railroad Park Road.

State Highway Bridge, Dunsmuir, California … aka Sacramento River Bridge … aka Pacific Highway Bridge. Dedicated in 1916, this concrete arch bridge is still in use spanning the Sacramento River.

Mt. Shasta, Cal., from Pacific Highway

State Highway Bridge, Dunsmuir, California. Mt. Shasta , Cal. from Pacific Highway.

Carole MacRobert Steele

Pacific Highway Bridge over Sacramento River, Dunsmuir, Ca and Mt. Shasta. Postmarked 1926 from Medford, Oregon. Lamp posts on bridge.

Pacific Highway Bridge over Sacramento River, Dunsmuir, 1940's.

Pacific Highway Bridge. 1960's view now in conjunction with I-5.

Mt. Shasta—The Mountain

Mount Shasta is known as California's "Mystic Mountain." For over one hundred years, psychics have written about this Shasta Valley peak which is shadowed in mystery and intrigue. There are stories of secret caverns lined with gold, odd lights shining on the slopes, bells ringing, and oddest of all ... tales of cities ten miles under the mountain where beings with supernatural powers live.

No one really knows how Shasta got it's name, but the mountain is a dormant volcano 14,162 feet in elevation. Scientist study and monitor it on a regular basis so the surrounding area can be given a warning ahead of a possible eruption. The mountain was built by repeated eruptions forming its four overlapping cones. It's the youngest of the volcanoes in the Cascade Range and the lower forty-eight States. It has five glaciers, as well as four hundred species of alpine plants.

Mind-boggling in its beauty, early travel logs describe those who see the mountain for the first time: "The snow-covered top of Shasta first strikes your vision. The snow cap seems like a ghost floating in space; then gradually you perceive a shadowy form beneath the huge mass of a mountain disclosed standing almost by itself in the plain." Poet Joaquin Miller wrote of the mountain: "Lonely as God and white as the winter moon." Indian tribes would not climb above the timberline because the "Great Spirit Who Dwells in this Mountain with His People are in a Tent." Mt. Shasta was unknown to the world until a Hudson Bay trapper recorded its presence in 1827.

Mt. Shasta from Pacific Highway. 1920's dirt road with photographer's car parked; his trunk strapped on back.

Mt. Shasta, Calif. From Pacific Highway. Early 1920's dirt road. Photographer's car with trunk strapped on back.

Photo of Pacific Highway between Sisson (Mt. Shasta City) and Dunsmuir, Calif. May, 1920. Crude dirt road and railing fence.

Mt. Shasta from Pacific Highway, Sacramento Canyon. Postmarked 1933 from Spokane. Graded dirt road and telephone poles.

Carole MacRobert Steele

Mt. Shasta and Pacific Highway, 1920's-30's. Road looks like packed dirt, but not paved; no white center line.

Mt. Shasta From Pacific Highway. Approximately 1930's.

Postmarked 1946 from Sacramento (1930s car parked) Message on back written while they were on the train: "So far have had a sleeper. I saw this mt. It sure was beautiful. We went halfway around it. Just go done eating. Am trying to write while train is going." Road is paved.

Carole MacRobert Steele

Mt. Shasta from Pacific Highway. Road is paved. Railroad tracks visible on the left middle; 1930's.

Postmarked 1946 from Dunsmuir. Message on back: "I thought you would like this photograph of Mt. Shasta. I stayed here at Shasta Springs and ate the food last night. This is very beautiful country. We are driving to the Northwest on a vacation trip." Road is paved. Railroad tracks on left.

Mt. Shasta from Pacific Highway. Postmarked 1949 from Mt. Shasta. Road is paved, but no center line. White road marker posts.

Carole MacRobert Steele

Mt. Shasta from Pacific Highway, 1940's. Paved with white center line. Several telephone poles.

Shasta Cascade Wonderland consists of eight counties: Butte, Lassen, Modoc, Plumas, Shasta, Siskiyou, Tehama, Trinity. A bounty of natural attractions with lakes, rivers, and scenic drives. The SCW Association started in 1938. 1940's car (same view as above), but now there are white highway posts on the right and a Highway 99 shield sign.

Mt. Shasta and Pacific Highway, 1940's. Road is paved with white center line; several cracks in the pavement.

Carole MacRobert Steele

Mt. Shasta from Pacific Highway postmarked 1941 from Yreka with Highway 99 shield sign. Sender's message: "Painted sign by side of highway here. Nice view eh?" There's a large sign way up on the road slightly visible on the right.

A Pictorial History of Highway 99: The Scenic Route   103

Postmarked 1931 from Mt. Shasta. Sender writes: "We are now in Shasta City. Are going to go to Lassen Nat'l Park and then home." Road is paved and showing two 1930's cars in background.

Carole MacRobert Steele

Highway 99 postmarked 1954 from Weed. Message: "Got to Weed. Having a nice trip. Nice and cool here. This Mt. Is still covered with snow." Road paved with broken white line.

Mt. Shasta from Pacific Highway, US 99 shield sign on the right. Paved with solid white line, 1940's.

Mt. Shasta 1940's paved road with solid white line. There's a sign on the side of the road that reads "Men and Equipment Working."

Mt. Shasta. 1940's Rainier Beer billboard on the far right at curve.

Carole MacRobert Steele

Mt. Shasta. 1950's four lane paved road with broken white lines. White guard rails and snow depth marker poles.

Pacific Highway and Mt. Shasta near Shasta Springs, Cal. 1930's. There is NO Shasta Springs Hotel sign.

Mt. Shasta, Calif. Same view as previous, but now the Shasta Springs Hotel sign is clearly visible on the right. Road paved; 1930's cars.

1930's close up view of Shasta Springs Hotel billboard which says: "One Minute" Open May 1. Cement bridge, road paved, no white center line.

Shasta Springs

At an altitude of 2,556 feet, Shasta Springs summer resort was located on the Sacramento River near Dunsmuir. Well known for its mineral baths, the resort was on the main line of the Southern Pacific Railroad. The Railroad promoted the resort by offering rides on the "Road to A Thousand Wonders." Early travel guides described Shasta Springs as: "Above the narrow canyon of the Sacramento on a little plateau carpeted with green lawns stand trim green and white cottages. Here bubbling Shasta Water is bottled and shipped all over the country." The natural springs located on the property became the source for water and beverages that became known as SHASTA brand soft drinks; and are still being sold today. Business waned in the 1920's, and by the 1950's the resort was closed and sold to the Saint Germain Foundation. It's currently closed to the general public. The bottling plant, train station, fountain and incline railroad are gone, but their ruins can be seen through the overgrowth of blackberry bushes.

Shasta Springs, 1930's. Shows the hotel and depot with the Railroad tracks in front. Waterfall and upper geyser spout visible in the middle.

Shasta Springs, Ca. 1940's. SHASTA SPRINGS sign on top of the Railroad station with the river in foreground.

Shasta Springs Lodge, Dunsmuir, 1940's. This lodge was located on top of the hill above the Springs.

76:—A Shasta Route Train near Mt. Shasta, Calif.

Southern Pacific Portland Express train, 1920's. A Shasta Route train near Mt. Shasta, Calif. If you chose not to drive the highway, you could opt to take this scenic train ride.

"MT. EDDY" FROM HIGHWAY "99 NEAR MT. SHASTA CITY. CALIF. J.H. EASTMAN B-1347

"Mt. Eddy" from Highway 99 near Mt. Shasta City. Mt. Eddy is the highest peak of the Trinity Mountains in Siskiyou and Trinity Counties. At an elevation 9,037 feet, it's the highest summit West of Interstate 5; named in honor of Olive Paddock Eddy who was the first woman to climb Mt. Shasta. She arrived from New York in 1856. It's original Wintu tribe name was "West Blaze Mountain." Photo is 1940's showing two paved lanes with solid white line.

Carole MacRobert Steele

Mt. Shasta City

Settled in the 1850's, the City is located on the lava flow base of Mt. Shasta for which it was named. In the 1880's, the City was called Sisson after J. H. Sisson who had donated the land to build the City. He was once the town postmaster and hotel/tavern owner. After a town vote, the name was changed to Mt. Shasta City in 1925. In the 1920's as tourist travel and the logging industry grew, cars on US 99 drove past the City's lumber mills, lumber yards, and log ponds. The area soon developed into a popular destination for sports enthusiasts, artists, professional people, naturalists, and religious sects.

Mt. Shasta City entrance arch. Written on the back of the card: "Black Beauty 15 miles away." Writer probably meant Black Butte; its peak visible in the distance. Billboard on the left says AUTO PARK with a sign pointing to Abrams lake; which is now a mobile home park on North Old Stage Road.

Mt. Shasta, Cal. 1930's showing the Pacific Highway leading into town. Gas station visible on right.

Carole MacRobert Steele

Mount Shasta. 1940's. Highway going through business district. Readable signs include: Veterans Club, Mt. Shasta Club, Park Hotel with dining room and coffee shop. Two gas pumps on the street and sidewalk with Black Butte in the distance.

Mt. Shasta, 1940's. Highway going down Main Street. Shows the Solari Hotel on the right with a Richfield gas station across the street. Black Butte peak visible.

Mount Shasta, California

1960's view of Mount Shasta City. Part of the caption on the back: "The ski bowl attracts thousands of skiers during ski season," Visible is a coffee shop on the corner with Montgomery Wards next door and Rexall Drug, Sprouse Ritz.

1952 date on back. Armstrong's Motel. John H. Gordon, Mt. Shasta City. Has garages.

Shasta Lodge at Mt. Shasta, Calif. Postmarked 1956 from Portland. Sender writes: "The trip home was wonderful. Notice drinking fountain in front—real spring water. The scenery is wonderfully refreshing." There is a stone fountain with a sign that says COLD. A sign that says Indian Jewelry—Curios. Another sign reads: THIS LODGE FOR SALE.

NEW MISSION MOTEL - HIGHWAY 99 - MT. SHASTA, CALIFORNIA

Mt. Shasta, Ca., New Mission Motel—Highway 99. Late 1940's or early 1950's. Lawn with chairs and swing.

Marilyn's Fine Foods early 1950's Highway 99 restaurant.

Marilyn's Restaurant 1960's. Changes in architecture and cement entrance steps walkway. Landmark of good eating and famous stage stop; is now a Mexican restaurant.

Carole MacRobert Steele

Civilian Conservation Corps Camp with Mt. Shasta in the background. Wooden sign reads: CAMP F-394 MT. SHASTA Company 978. 1930's card captioned: Mt. Shasta from CCC Camp, Highway 99

This CCC camp was located in the Shasta National Forest near on Sims Road near Castella and was known as Camp Sims from 1934-39. Camp Sims was a haven to boys from Company 978 who came from the San Francisco Bay Area to work. Administered by the US Army and the U.S. Forest Service, the CCC was in charge of projects such as fire fighting, building lookouts, and constructing highways and campgrounds.

The CCC started in the 1930s by President Franklin Roosevelt putting needy young men to work during the Depression years. Part of their paycheck was sent home to the parents. Many CCC projects from the 1930's are still being effectively used today.

Black Butte

The lava dome known as Black Mountain stands in the shadow of Mt. Shasta near Weed. "Butte" is the French word meaning "ridge." It was originally named Muir's Peak after the famous naturalist John Muir who loved the area. Muir spent days and nights camped alone near Mt. Shasta basking in its beauty. On seeing Mt. Shasta for the first time, he wrote: "My blood turned to wine, and I have not been weary since." U.S. 99 cuts around the Eastern flanks of Black Butte peak.

Black Butte, Cal. Pacific Highway. 1920's crude dirt road.

Black Butte, Ca on Pacific Highway; shows a car on crude dirt road. Postmarked 1928 from Black Butte, Ca.

Black Butte from Pacific Highway Aug. 8, 1935. Message: "Just before we arrived at Weed, Cal." Road is paved.

Black Butte 1930's paved road with center white line and white fence railing. Road crosses over railroad tracks.

Black Butte 1930's paved road with no white line. Looks like smoke at top on backside of Butte.

"Black Butte"
Highway 99

Black Butte Highway 99 paved with broken white line, 1940's. Roadside billboard is blank. Lookout visible on top of Butte.

Black Butte down Highway 99; 1950's. Fire lookout on Butte. Billboard advertises RAINIER BEER. Previous card shows billboard is blank.

Black Butte from Highway 99, 1950's paved road with solid white line.

Black Butte Pacific Highway, 1930's paved road with no line; snow.

Black Butte with lots of snow. 1930's.

Black Butte from US 99. Postmarked 1937 from Mt. Shasta. Message: "You'd love the camp now. Lots of changes. Lots of snow on Shasta."

Black Butte, Calif. 1950's. Paved road with broken white line.

Snow Plow Keeping California State Highways Open at Shasta-Weed. 1930's-40's. Snow plows were used as early as 1930's.

City of Mount Shasta with nearby Black Butte, 1950's. Shows Highway 99 winding through town and skirting the base of the Butte.

Mt. Shasta from Black Butte Lookout; postmarked 1947. Black Butte Fire Lookout was a U. S. Forest Service tower on the summit built in the early 1930's. It was destroyed by a storm in 1962, and a new one was built in 1963. The lookout was in operation until 1973 when the building was removed by helicopter to a new location in 1975. Only the concrete foundation remains atop the Butte. A two and a half mile trail leads to the summit at an elevation of 6,334 feet.

Carole MacRobert Steele

Black Butte Lookout, Cal. 1930's.

Black Butte Mountain, 1960's. Complete section of Interstate 5/U. S. 99 freeway near Mt. Shasta City. Black Butte in the background. Four lanes and a 65 mph sign visible.

Pinehurst Auto Park on Pacific Highway, South of Weed; 1930's. Road is paved.

CHAPTER V

Weed to the Oregon State Line

⟨∞⟩

Weed

At an elevation 3,466 feet and located at the junction of U.S. 97, Weed was described in early travel guides as "A lumber town bleak and rough-looking laying, in a hill-rimmed hollow; brush sweeping down to encroach on weather-beaten house and rickety fences. South of Weed, US 99 winds over rounded hills dotted with pines."

Pioneer Abner Weed, the town founder, had purchased the Siskiyou Lumber and Mercantile Mill and 280 acres of land in 1897 for $400.00. In 1913, the town had a population of fifteen hundred; mostly males employed in the sawmill. At times, things got rough with shootings and brawls. A Redding newspaper described it as a dingy dangerous town and calling it Sodom and Gomorrah. The town of Weed today is a town with charm, clean air, pine vistas, and Mt. Shasta!

1920's entrance arch WELCOME To WEED. Weed Hotel and Weed Garage on the right with the Golden State Hotel on the left.

View of highway entering Weed. The WEED sign on the right was erected by the California State Automobile Association. Postmarked 1948 from Weed.

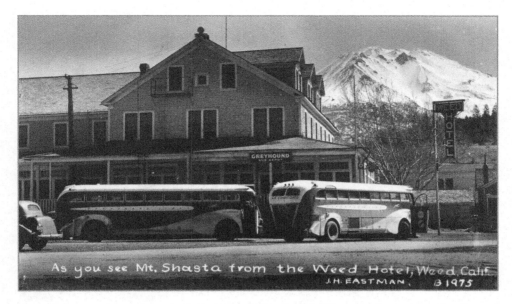

"As you see Mt. Shasta from the Weed Hotel, Weed, Calif." Postmarked 1952. Greyhound buses at Greyhound Bus Depot. Message: "It is 4:30 a.m. now and must board bus."

Deer Mt. Lodge, Weed, Calif. 1950's.

Mt. Shasta from Weed 1940's. Log Cabin Hotel and Cafe with Standard gas station next door. Coca-Cola sign on the left says Log Cabin Hotel parking.

Mt. Shasta from Mountain Service Station (Standard Oil Products) 1940's. This is the gas station next door to the Log Cabin Hotel shown in previous postcard. Shows three gas pumps and lubrication building to the right; Carl Phelps, owner.

Carole MacRobert Steele

Mt. Shasta and "Pilgrim's Rest Modern Cabins" Weed 1950's.

Mt. Shasta from Weed. Pilgrim's Rest Auto Camp. 27 cabins, store and groceries; meats, soft drinks, tobacco. Gas pumps on the far left. Pilgrim's Rest is/was located at 88 S. Weed Blvd on Highway 99. In the 1950's it was a motor court of little cottages with a residence and front office. In 1950, the cottages on the upper level were removed; and eventually all were removed. The motel section was built with two apartments. Fifteen rooms were built on the lower section. It's now the Hi-Lo Motel and RV Park located on three acres with forty-one rooms, four apartments, restaurant, and Richfield gas.

Weed, Calif. - Shasta View Gift Shop and Studio; Aaron Thomas, owner. Cafe next door. Souvenirs visible in the window. FREE PHOTO sign on roof.

The road to Mt. Shasta near Yreka, Calif. 1920's with visible dust kicked up by the car driving on the dirt road. Very early view of the Pacific Highway.

Carole MacRobert Steele

Shamrock Auto Court 5 miles S. of Yreka, Ca. On US 99. 1940's with Mt. Shasta visible in the distance. Written on back: "Electric pump to furnish the water from a 90' well. Good water. 7 acres of ground. Pine and oak trees, 10 cabins. Store and 6 rooms in home all furnished. Velvet rugs and everything complete. Oil burner for heater. 3 gas pumps." This description sounds like the auto court was for sale.

The Shamrock Dining Room and Cocktail Lounge five miles So. Highway 99 off highway on Shamrock Rd. 1960's. Closed in the 1970's; never reopened and still stands vacant.

Yreka, California

The Seat of Siskiyou County, Yreka is derived from the word "Wy-ree-kah" … a Shasta Indian name meaning "mountain." It's located sixteen miles from the Oregon border, and is the largest town between Redding and Medford. Blocks of gracious old white houses, shaded by locust trees, line Highway 99, which was Yreka's "Main Street." It was the capital of the short-lived State of Jefferson which claimed to be the 49th State in the Union. State of Jefferson devotees are still trying to get that to become a reality. In the 1850's gold was discovered here, and the County Courthouse housed an exhibit of various forms of gold. A few years ago, that gold was brazenly stolen from the exhibit. I don't think it was ever recovered.

Yreka, Calif. Main Street 1930's. The Yreka Inn is on the left. Across the street is a Richfield gas station ,Yreka Auto Park, and Cafe.

MAIN STREET, YREKA, CALIFORNIA.   ON PACIFIC HIGHWAY   6024

Yreka, Calif. Main Street on Pacific Highway. Yreka Inn on left; 1930s.

"Yreka Inn" Yreka, Calif.   Eastman's Studio B-1478

Yreka Inn, Yreka, Calif. 1940's. Touted to be the grandest hotel between San Francisco and Portland, the Inn was built in 1925 by the Weaver Brothers. Constructed of concrete, it had one hundred two rooms with an adjoining restaurant, dinner house, and ballroom. It was considered a first class hotel popular with tourists and locals, but unable to compete with low cost motels, the Inn was razed in 1975, and a bank was built on the site.

Entering Yreka, Calif. as seen from the North going South toward Weed, 1930's.

The home of California Senator Randolph Collier; 551 Main Street, Yreka, California. The home was built in 1932 and is still standing.

Randolph Collier (1902–1983) was elected State Senator from 1938-1963. He was Chairman of the Senate Transportation Committee for twenty-two years and ruled it with an iron hand. When Interstate 5 was being built, it was going to be routed from Grenada to Hornbrook, but he was able to get it redirected

Carole MacRobert Steele

to pass through Yreka, thus saving the town from dying due to lack of tourist business. He became known as the: Father of Freeways, Mr. California Highway, and Sage of the Siskiyous ... for his expert planning and financing of California's highways in the 1940's.

His home was Art Deco in style and painted a cream color with green trim; but later painted pink. When we lived in Yreka in the 1970's, it was still painted pink. It always stood out as one of the grander homes on Main Street. The house once had a swimming pool in the backyard. During the Depression years, a local man was paid $1.00 a day (and happy to get it) to dig out the ground where the pool was to be. The house still stands, but has lost its glory.

Shasta River on State Highway near Yreka, Calif. Message written on back dated 9-25-1927: "Arrived here a few days ago camping on the Shasta River where Robert is having some fine salmon fishing, big fellows 20-30 lbs. All the camp has fish dinners." Card shows the old original Pacific Highway dirt road along the Shasta River.

Shasta River Canyon is known today as Highway 263 which crosses the Klamath River and enters Shasta River Canyon eight miles North of Yreka. The road was first built in 1914 and realigned in 1929. Taken from a 1931 news article: "Construction started on new road in 1930 high on the side of Shasta Canyon and replacing the crooked and narrow road at the bottom of the Canyon—a striking example of the manner in which modern engineering are tearing down mountainsides in their effort to build highways straight, wide. and safe."

In 1914, nine and a half miles of road had been constructed North of Yreka where the Shasta and Klamath Rivers join. The road was sixteen feet wide with two-lane directional traffic and 137 curves. It was a thirty mile per hour road with guard rails installed on dangerous curves. By the 1920's it had become obsolete due to the increased traffic and was simply too steep, narrow, and windy to be safe.

The new alignment was called Highway 99. There were five bridges built on a four and a half mile stretch which helped shorten the road by two miles. It took 249 tons of TNT dynamite to blow up enough earth to reduce the curves to just twenty-five.

When it came time for another realignment in the 1950's, the Shasta Canyon was totally rejected as being suitable for a four-lane highway; thus Interstate 5 was built high above the canyon walls.

Highway Along the Shasta River. Shasta River on State Highway near Yreka. 1920's original Pacific Highway dirt road.

Pacific Highway and Shasta River, Ca. Postmarked 1926. The road crosses the truss bridge and keeps going through the canyon; shows guard rail.

Shasta Canyon, Ca. near Yreka. 1920's showing the highway up above on the right.

See previous image which is the same, but different. This is a later 1930's view. The road now has a white railing, but is still dirt as it comes down off the hill. Mt. Shasta in background.

Over the Shasta River near Yreka. 1930's with bridge. Original highway visible on the canyon floor along the river.

Cut and Bridge. Mt. Shasta Canyon near Yreka. View looking North. Written on back: "Cut 110 ft. One year to cut through each cut. Steam shovel. Road built 8 miles to get shovel to cut." 1930's.

On the Pacific Highway near Yreka, Dry Gulch Bridge 1930's. Dry Gulch Bridge was built in the 1930's as part of the major realignment and improvement of Highway 99 from Yreka to the Klamath River in Shasta River Canyon. Located North of Yreka, this bridge crosses Dry Gulch Creek which flows into the Shasta River along Highway 263, which was once Highway 99. Unfortunately during the road improvements of the 1970's, the open sides and built-in benches on the bridge were filled in. Its beauty can best be observed looking up at it from the canyon floor on the original old highway.

Single arch bridge Shasta Canyon near Yreka, Calif. 1930's.

Pacific Highway Shasta River Canyon, Cal. 1930's old highway along the River showing white railings.

The Great Shasta River Bridge, Pacific Highway, 1930's. Crude dirt road leading onto the Bridge entrance. Old highway visible below that followed the River.

Shasta River Canyon near Yreka. Old highway visible below following the curves of the River, 1950's.

The photograph bears the handwritten caption: "The Steel Bridge 252 ft. to the water. Highest on the Pacific Highway. 1513 FT."

The Steel Bridge … highest on Pacific Highway; officially named Pioneer Bridge. The old highway is visible below in the Shasta River Canyon. This cantilevered Warren deck truss bridge is so tall that the California State Capitol building would fit under it. Highway 263 over the Shasta River is a North/South highway between Yreka and the Oregon State line as it passes through Shasta River Canyon. Interstate 5 remains high on a ridge well above the old highway. The Pioneer Bridge was dedicated in 1931 and a bronze plaque was placed on a granite boulder with the words: "To the pioneers of stage and team who blazed this trail and crossed this stream … this bridge is dedicated to you."

Pioneer Bridge, Pacific Highway near Yreka.

The Steel Bridge ... highest on Pacific Highway, 1930's. Old dirt highway visible along the river.

Pioneer Bridge, Shasta Canyon near Yreka, 1930's. Old dirt highway visible below along the river.

Pioneer Bridge, Shasta Canyon, Yreka. Dirt road below with steel trestle bridge, 1930's.

Steel Bridge, Pacific Highway, Northern California, 252 feet high, 1930's. On the left corner trees are planted, and the bronze plaque that was placed 8-29-1931 is visible.

Pacific Highway, Northern California. Tree is now bigger than shown in previous image, and a sign is now next to it that says SHASTA RIVER. Road is paved with white center line, 1940's. View looks North.

Pacific Highway on Klamath River. "Clam-ath" is the name given by the Chinook Indians to a sister tribe of the Modoc Indians who called themselves MakLaks; "the encamped people." 1920's old dirt highway and trestle bridge. Highway 99, now 263, crossed the Klamath River and entered Shasta River Canyon eight miles North of Yreka. The original highway built in 1914 was realigned in 1929. To achieve this, tons of dirt and rock were blasted to make room for the five bridges that would need to be built to cross the rivers. The new highway was completed in 1931. The original trestle bridge is gone, and the open railings of the current bridge are now solid walls. This stretch of Old 99 is still in use by locals.

Pacific Highway on Klamath River, 1920's dirt highway follows the River.

Klamath River Bridge Pacific Highway. Steel trestle bridge is visible and was replaced by the new concrete bridge leading to Yreka. The road is paved.

Pacific Highway, Klamath River. Steel trestle bridge is now gone from view as seen in previous image, 1930's.

Over the Klamath River near Yreka. Same bridge as last view. Sign on bridge says KLAMATH RIVER. This view is heading North, 1940's.

Camp Lowe, Klamath River. Located thirteen miles North of Yreka on the Klamath River, Camp Lowe was an anglers paradise for fishing steelhead trout and salmon. Cars drove across the narrow bridge to get the cabins and campground on the other side of the River. Camp Lowe appealed to passing motorists and locals as a scenic place for recreation and rest.

Camp Lowe, Klamath River, 1930's. Entrance to Camp Lowe. The cabins are across the bridge. Visible is a Richfield gas station and the sign reads: ENTRANCE CAMP LOWE. Pacific Highway, shown in front of Camp Lowe, travels North to the town of Hornbrook. The bridge is now gone; only it's stone pilings and timber remain. Some Camp buildings of bygone days are still scattered along the banks of the River.

Hornbrook, Calif. looking South towards Yreka, pre-1914. Shows the Square Deal gas station with the Ladies Parlor building behind. Next to the gas station is a cafe with a sign that says EATS. Hornbrook was established in 1825 as a stage stop for travelers heading to Oregon. At an altitude of 2115 feet, the town lies downhill across Cottonwood Creek. The town is described in a 1930's travel guide: "Old brick structures, store buildings with wooden awnings, and a handful of shanties shadowed by shaggy Black Walnut trees." In 2018 Hornbrook suffered a devastating wildfire that burned several homes and thousands of acres of surrounding forested hills. Luckily the downtown was saved.

Near Moore's Auto Camp, two miles North of Hornbrook, Calif.; pre-1914. Shows dirt road Pacific Highway crossing the Klamath River and a steel trestle-style bridge.

A mountain road near Yreka, Calif. This is actually the road at nearby Scott Valley, but it gives reader an idea of how crude the roads were in the pre-1920 era. Road is described as, "unpassable; not even jack-assable."

California/Oregon State Border, 1920's. Shows the dirt highway coming South from Oregon. Triangle-shaped sign says CALIFORNIA STATE LINE and SISKIYOU COUNTY LINE. Large square sign gives regulations notices to visiting motorists. Photographer's car parked alongside.

Pacific Highway is paved with white center line, 1930's. Sign on the left reads STATE HIGHWAY ENTERING CALIFORNIA. Under it is a white shield sign that reads OREGON U.S. 99. Sign on the right side says CALIFORNIA STATE LINE.

Oregon

The All Year Scenic Pacific Highway—U.S. 99—Takes You to the Heart of Oregon's Great Vacationland.

CHAPTER VI

California/Oregon State Line to Ashland

LEAVING OREGON 1950's road sign made of logs and lumber. "We hope you enjoyed your visit ... come again."

OREGON Song and lyrics by S. H. Logan and Hazel E. Logan; copyright 1931. "There's a land out West we all love best" and ends, "this land of dreams … joy of living do we find here, Oregon, for thee we cheer."

Carole MacRobert Steele

That Dear Old Flivver

Once she was straight
  And full of pep,
Had a fast gait
  And kept her step.

Now she is faded
  And beginning to wrinkle,
Her eyes look jaded
  And refuse to twinkle.

Her time is not long
  Cause her lungs are weak,
Her voice once strong
  Is reduced to a squeak.

My eyes they fill
  When I'm tempted to part,
Because she still
  Holds a place in my heart.

She carried me to hunt,
  She carried me to marry,
Without a single grunt
  Or suggestion to tarry.

Along the countryside
  Or down by the river,
I've enjoyed every ride
  In that dear old "flivver".

KING A. WOODBURN.

"That Dear Old Flivver" by King A. Woodburn, 1920's. "Along the countryside or down by the river, I've enjoyed every ride in that dear old "flivver." Shows the way travel was in the 1920's with the whole family. A flivver is defined as a cheap car in bad condition.

Siskiyou Mountains

Pronounced Siss-kee-you, it's probably from the Cree Indian word Siskiyawatin, meaning "spotted horse."

In 1828 Archibald McLeod of the Hudson Bay Co. crossed the Siskiyou Mountains in a snow storm and lost his animals; including a bob-tailed horse. His Canadian followers named the place "Pass of the Siskiyou's." The Siskiyou's run East to West from the Cascades to the Coast Range.

1920's Oregon/California State Line. Siskiyou Mts. looking North. Triangle signs in foreground say OREGON STATE LINE/JACKSON COUNTY. Other sign says REGISTRATION OFFICE. Photographer's car visible. Pacific Highway was the first road over the Siskiyou's and completed in 1915. The first town encountered once in California was Hilt, which began as a railroad town and then became a mill town.

1930's Pacific Highway, California/Oregon State line. Signs say OREGON STATE LINE/JACKSON COUNTY. White sign says OREGON.

1950's Oregon/California State line, Pacific Highway; paved with white center line. Sign on left says OREGON STATE LINE, California State Automobile Association. Sign on right says STATE BOUNDARY ENTERING OREGON with an Oregon US 99 shield below.

1920's Pacific Highway, Siskiyou Mts. Crude dirt road with a little snow.

Same view as previous. 1920's Pacific Highway at Summit of Siskiyou Mts., Ashland, Oregon . Photographer's car and two ladies standing on the right.

Pilot Rock near Ashland, Oregon postmarked 1912. Pilot Knob, a "guardian sentinel," was a landmark loved by pioneers and Indians; a monument of guidance to get over the mountains. It's been described as, "a great massive rock pointing skyward with all its beauty of form visible at a great distance."

Summit—Siskiyou Mts. Elevation 4466 feet; 1940's snow scene. Siskiyou Summit is the highest point on Highway 99 and a favorite stopping point for truckers needing a rest after the long ascent. At the top there's plenty of room to pull off and park to make safety checks or just take a break.

Highest point on the Pacific Highway, 4516 feet, Siskiyou Mts. Triangle sign reads: STATE HIGHWAY SUMMIT-SISKIYOU ELEVATION 4516. Two-story log home to the right; other smaller buildings on the road.

Carole MacRobert Steele

On the Pacific Highway at Summit of Siskiyou Mts., Oregon. Sign on roof reads SUMMIT RANCH, elev. 4522 feet; Highest Point on the Pacific Highway. A picnic table is visible. Summit Ranch Lodge and Service Station was built in the early 1920's. It welcomed travelers by offering cabins and a restaurant that advertised "home cooking." There was a large garden in the summer which provided vegetables for the restaurant. Summit Ranch included several businesses. In 1930, a Richfield Service Station was built providing gas, tires, supplies and, repair service. The station had elaborate restrooms with a lounge and landscaped parking. There was also a confectionery store, lunch counter, and tea room.

Pacific Highway and photographer's car. Road compacted, not paved.

Pacific Highway Siskiyou Mts … crude road, white guard rails, 1939.

Pacific Highway on the Siskiyou's, 1939. Road is paved.

THE SISKIYOU SUMMIT COFFEE SHOP, OREGON - EASTMAN'S STUDIO B-5796
ELEVATION 4466 FT.

1948 Siskiyou Summit Coffee Shop, Oregon. Elev. 4466 feet. SHELL gas sign on the roof. Large COCA-COLA sign visible. Sender's message on back: "Our house on the hill. The drive begins at the gas pump. The little house on the point was the weather station. They have discontinued it. Mt. Ashland is just off the left side. We haven't been over these mountains, but around them." The coffee shop opened in 1946. It also provided a towing service, and buses stopped to let passengers have a meal and rest. During winter storms the cafe was warm and inviting with its windows steamed up from the hot coffee and food.

State Line Service, Hilt, California on Highway 99. Located on the sunny side of the Siskiyou's, this 1950's view show they served Mobil Gas, liquor, sandwiches, and Frosty ice cream. An 1895 steam engine is on display. When the highway was reconstructed, a new summit was created South of the old one, and the Summit Coffee Shop opened in 1946 (see previous image). This building is now a liquor store selling to Oregonians who can't buy liquor in their State.

Ruby's Kitchen was located on the Oregon side of the Summit eleven miles South on Highway 99. In the 1940's, Bob and Mickey Wilson were the owners. Known as a "greasy spoon" and truck stop cafe, they served hot lunches. It burned down on August 13, 1955.

Siskiyou Summit Oregon Centennial Stockade. Signs on the posts read: 417th Reserve Engine Brigade—Medford. The Welcome Booth Stockade was opened on May 18, 1959 for visitors coming to Oregon for its 100th Centennial celebration. Located at the top of the Summit, it was built by eighty Army Reserves as a replica of an early day fort. Southern Oregon College students manned it twelve hours a day starting at 8 a.m. The students named it the "Welcome to Oregon Center" and offered restrooms and Centennial literature. The Stockade had sentry posts with telescopes. The "Centennial 59ers" sold merchandise for $1.00 to fund building of the Stockade.

Pacific Highway, Siskiyou Mts. Oregon,1930's and snow.

Top of Siskiyou Grade, 1939. Shows snow, people, and cars. Road is paved.

Summit of Siskiyou Mts. US 99 in Oregon between Yreka, Calif. and Ashland, Ore. 1940's, snow.

Carole MacRobert Steele

Nina's Cedar Tree Tavern, Siskiyou Summit, Hiway 99, Ashland, Ore. "Enjoy hearty western hospitality over the huge rustic bar, hand-wrought in one piece from local Oregon cedar." This tavern had pinball machines and a jukebox, 1950's.

Pacific Highway near Ashland, Ore. Dated 1923, view of crude dirt road and a pre-1920 car; probably the photographer's.

Pacific Highway, Siskiyou Mts., Oregon. 1930's cars coming down the grade towards Ashland. Photographer's car, white guard rail.

Pacific Highway Siskiyou Mts. Dated 1925. Crude road, photographers' car.

Pacific Highway through Siskiyou's, mid-1920's.

Watering autos, Pacific Highway at Siskiyou, Oregon; checking radiators. Pre-1920 crude dirt road. Six people in the rear car.

Pacific Highway Siskiyou Mts., pre-1920. Very early crude single lane gravel road coming down the grade toward Ashland. RR tracks in foreground. Billboard reads: Ashland 14 mi. - the Carlsbad of America. Lithia Soda and Sulphur Springs.

Pacific Highway near Medford, Ore. Same view as previous card and billboard reads the same. Photographer's car is parked.

Carole MacRobert Steele

Same view as previous card, 1930's. This is the famous "Siskiyou Loop" one of the most photographed spots on the Pacific Highway. The billboard is now gone. Two shacks have been built and guard rail erected. Photographer's car on the right.

Panoramic similar to last view. "Siskiyou Loop on Pacific Highway" 1930's. Shack visible on the right.

Pacific Highway on the Siskiyou's, 1930's. Another view of "The Loop"

Ribbon rock on Pacific Highway in Siskiyou Mts. near Ashland; late teens. Shows how the mountain had to be cut away to construct the highway. Crude one lane road. Trees cut in the forest during construction a hundred years ago have now all grown back now.

Carole MacRobert Steele

Pacific Highway near Ashland, Ore. postmarked 1947 from Grants Pass. Sender's message: "We are having a grand trip in Grants Pass today. We came over this beautiful drive coming down out of the Siskiyou Mts the other day. We sleep out under the stars every night; in fact, we're right out of doors all the time. Southern Oregon looks much like California." Crude one lane dirt road.

Pacific Highway in Siskiyou Mts., 1920's.

Pacific Highway in Siskiyou Mts. 1930's with white guard rail.

184   *Carole MacRobert Steele*

Sign on road "Siskiyou Camp Entrance 800 ft. above. Camping. Warm Cabins." Located a couple of miles on the Oregon side down from Summit Ranch. Advertisement reads: "Comfortable bed with or without bedding; good meals."

Siskiyou Camp sign ENTRANCE. 1930's car, gas pump. Cabins visible on right.

Cabin at Siskiyou Camp,1930's. 16 miles South of Ashland.

Siskiyou Camp, 16 miles South of Ashland, Ore. 1930s. Shows a lot of pictures of women on the walls. Crude homemade chairs made from trees.

Carole MacRobert Steele

The Pacific Highway at Siskiyou, Ore. Pre-1920 crude dirt road. Houses and buildings visible.

Siskiyou, Ore. 1940's with white guard rail; train on the tracks.

Pacific Highway Siskiyou Mts., Siskiyou, Ore. White guard rail; town visible in distance; road paved with white center line.

Pacific Highway Siskiyou Mts. 1920's with white guard rail. Town in distance just around the curve.

Carole MacRobert Steele

Callahan's Siskiyou Lodge, 1950's near Steinman Loop. Sign reads: CAFE/ROOMS. Arrow sign points to the Siskiyou Room and Lounge. A dog lays in front.

Oregon native Don Callahan dreamed of opening a lodge in the Siskiyou's. After his duty in WW11, he sold a small herd of sheep in 1944 to buy land on Highway 99 ten miles South of Ashland. With the help of friends, he worked tirelessly chiseling out solid rock on a sunny hillside to build his wood and stone lodge. Siskiyou Lodge opened in 1947 with a dining room, eight stools, and five tables ... serving skiers, hikers, travelers, and locals.

In 1964 the original site was condemned to make way for the new Interstate 5 right-of-way. Don Callahan bought a bigger piece of land a short distance up the highway and below the summit. It reopened in 1965. This new site had been part of the old village of Siskiyou. Callahan's was completely destroyed by fire in 2006 and a new and bigger lodge was built that continues to serve customers.

1950's Siskiyou Lodge, eight miles South of Ashland on Highway 99. "Complete lodging accommodations. Sleep and dine in the Siskiyou Mts." In this view, the cafe sign has been moved to the left and a new and bigger VACANCY sign is in front.

CALLAHAN'S RESTAURANT

1960's Callahan's Restaurant—Top of the Siskiyou's. Interstate 5 at Mt. Ashland interchange South of Ashland, Oregon.

Same view as above, but winter scene with deep snow. Mobile home parked on the right.

Pacific Highway crossing itself and the Southern Pacific Railroad, Siskiyou Mts., Ore. 1920's. The Siskiyou Loop Horseshoe dirt road with white guard rail located nine miles South of Ashland. The old landmark known as Steinman Crossing was called "Loop The Loop" and "The Over and Under." It was/is a 360 degree loop that crosses over the adjacent railroad tracks. It's the only bridge in Oregon where the road goes both over and under the concrete deck girder built in 1914. It was named after Ben Steinman; a Sacramento jeweler and friend of Southern Pacific railroad officials. In 1940, a new and gentler grade was realigned on Highway 99; however, this section of original highway was kept open to traffic, and you can still drive the "loop" today known as Old Siskiyou Highway.

"Loop the Loop" Pacific Highway, Siskiyou Mts. Steinman Crossing. Sender's 1927 messages reads: "On the way down, and it's all down all right too, besides looping the loop. Wonderful to look back at when one gets way down." The railroad tracks go under the bridge on the left.

Pacific Highway, 1920's. Shows the Steinman railroad crossing trestle bridge on the far right.

The Circle Loop on Pacific Highway in the Siskiyous, Oregon. Railroad water tower visible on far left by the tracks.

Concrete bridge on Pacific Highway, Siskiyou Mts near Ashland; pre-1919. Steinman railroad crossing and train. Crude dirt road on left; car goes over the bridge.

Pacific Highway bridge at Steinman in Siskiyou Mts., Oregon. Pacific Highway crossing itself; cement bridge. Postmarked 1919 from Medford, Oregon, message reads: "Just to let you know that we are still traveling. Had bad roads up to Grants Pass. Are getting better tomorrow. We are going to cross the Siskiyou's." Two signs on bridge read POST BILLS. Road on left improved a little from above card image.

Pacific Highway crosses itself and Southern Pacific Railroad, Siskiyou Mts. 1920's car on the bridge; train on the tracks.

Loop in Pacific Highway, Siskiyou Mts. 1930's road now paved with center white line.
Train on tracks; train water tower visible in background.

CHAPTER VII

Ashland

Ashland, Oregon, at an elevation of 1,895 feet, was once referred to as "The Venice of the West," and "Where the Palm Meets the Pine." Located on the California-Oregon Trail, the town was called Ashland Mills in 1871. The railroad arrived in 1887, and by 1900, it was the largest town in the Rogue Valley. Because of the town's famous curative mineral springs, it became widely known as a health resort. Other tourist attractions included the hundred acre Lithia Park and the Oregon Shakespearean Festival; America's first Elizabethan theater. Tourism still continues to be Ashland's main draw.

Boulevard Ave. Ashland, Ore. This is Siskiyou Blvd. pre-1920. Horse and buggy visible on the road. Very small new trees planted in center dirt/grass area. Road appears to be paved.

Entering Ashland, Ore. 1920's car visible. Center trees are bigger now. (Siskiyou Blvd. aka Highway 99, is the main street of Ashland).

Ashland, Ore. 1940's aerial view showing Southern Oregon College of Education (large building in the center). This college began as an academy in 1872. By 1926 it was called Southern Oregon Normal School. In 1939 it was renamed Southern Oregon College of Education; primarily as an institution to train teachers. Name changes continued in 1956 when it was called Southern Oregon College; Southern Oregon State College in 1975, and finally Southern Oregon University in 1995.

1940's Southern Oregon College of Education, Ashland, Oregon on Siskiyou Blvd.

1930's Ashland showing people drinking from the downtown Plaza Lithia Water fountain. Discovered in 1907, Ashland's lithium-laced and naturally carbonated water flows from a spring near the town. "Lithia Water" became famous for its healing powers as people flocked to Ashland to bathe in it, drink it, and cook with it. The foul-tasting water can still be sipped from the restored fountain at the Plaza on Main Street.

Ashland Plaza in 1940's-50's. Ore. US 99 shield sign visible on the center grassy area. Lithia Water fountain and City Hall visible to the far right.

Ashland Lithia Auto Camp

Located just west of downtown, the city of Ashland, in 1908, set aside ninety acres of city property along Ashland Creek as a park. From a nearby mineral spring, a pipe was built to carry the healing waters into the park. As a result, a health resort developed with people traveling to partake of the waters. By 1915 the City decided an auto camp was needed at this site to accommodate the increase in travelers. This FREE public auto camp declared itself to be the "finest on the Pacific Highway—"a modern beauty spot." By 1923, the Camp realized a fifty cent daily fee was needed to keep out "undesirables." Soon, a store and a few cabins with amenities were added as campers wanted to bring less equipment. Cabins could be built for as little as $200.00 and paid off in a season or two. Boasting luxury accommodations, it became one of the most visited camps on the Pacific Highway; bringing in $800.00 a month in revenue. It advertised three different kinds of mineral water, a children's playground, wading pools, cabins with kitchenettes, gas stoves, electric lights, laundry service, and a comfort station. In 1930 twenty more cabins were added, and eventually it was called the Lithia Auto Court and survived into the 1950's. Today, the Auto Camp Store is now used for the office of the Ashland Parks and Recreation. Only one of the original cabins still stands.

Lithia Auto Camp "Entrance to Free Auto Camp, Ashland, Ore" pre-1920.

Auto Camp Ground, Ashland, ore. Pre-1920; tents visible on the right.

Carole MacRobert Steele

"All the Comforts of Home at Ashland Free Auto Campground, Lithia Park." 1920's era shows Dad putting water in the radiator while Mom brings over a basin of water for washing up. The lady by the tents holds a coffee pot while three kids sit on a canvas camp cot. The other two kids are preparing food. They're staying at campsite #8. A man with his car is at campsite #9. A wood storage box is attached to the car's running board.

Ashland Auto Camp, 1925, Lithia Free Auto Camp. Several picnic tables are visible; wood storage box on the running board.

Entrance to Auto Camp, Ashland, Ore. 1930's. Shows the Lithia Park store/cafe selling refreshments, groceries, accessories.

Lithia Springs Auto Camp, Ashland, Ore. Modern Cabins. Shows little wood cabins and a courtyard, 1930's.

Carole MacRobert Steele

Lithia Auto Court (same view as previous, but a different angle). Cabins and improved courtyard and driveway. Clubhouse building. 1940's.

CHAPTER VIII

Ashland to Medford

Mountain View Motel, South Entrance, Ashland, Oregon 1940's. Highway 99 and 25 mph sign visible. Motel has garages, a courtyard with grass, and patio furniture.

White Cabin Auto Court, Ashland, Oregon, late 1930's. Located at 1520 Siskiyou Blvd. Shows the motel office, landscaping, rock wall, and lamp posts.

White Cabin Auto Court., Ashland, Oregon. Cabins with garages, nice rock wall, lamp posts.

At White Cabin Camp, Ashland. 1930's close-up view of cabins with garages. Each with a brick chimney.

1960's view of the White Motel, Hiway 99, So. Ashland. Caption reads: As you enter beautiful Rogue River Valley, lovely grounds, fully equipped modern units, swimming pool, free TV, electric heat, kitchenettes. Inset shows the pool. This motel is now gone.

Carole MacRobert Steele

Ashland Motel — Ashland, Oregon
Four of our 32 New Units ☆ On U.S. 99 ☆ 17 Miles North of California
"Luxury Without Extravagance"

Ashland Motel, Ashland, Oregon. "Four of our 32 new units on U. S. 99; 17 miles North of California." "Luxury Without Extravagance." 1940's. Units have garages and a grassy courtyard in front.

RATH'S MOTEL
One Block South of "OMAR'S" Hwy. #99
ASHLAND, OREGON

Rath's Motel, 1 Block South of Omar's—Hwy 99, Ashland, 1940's. Cabins with garages and landscaped grounds. Established in 1947, Omar's is Ashland's oldest and longest continuously operating restaurant between Redding and Portland. Omar's was built by Omer and Hazel Hill on the former site of Berkeley Hot Springs. Their popular little roadhouse was located at 1380 Siskiyou Blvd. The sign-maker misspelled Omer's name, so they just kept the name as Omar's! Travelers on Highway 99 were served the house specialties; chicken and steak. The restaurant started out with just a counter and stools, but in 1952 they added a dining room. A year later a lounge and bar was added; making it Ashland's first public cocktail lounge. The Hills sold out in 1956, and the restaurant remains in business operating as Omar's

1950's Vans Motel and Cafe, 4 miles S. on US 99, Ashland. 11 new modern units, TV, electric kitchens, tiled showers, wall-to-wall carpets. Cafe with home cooking. Two Flying A gas pumps with highway in foreground.

Jackson's Mineral Springs. Southern Pacific Railroad and Pacific Highway, Ashland, Ore. 1920. Shows paved highway going by the springs spouting steam.

Carole MacRobert Steele

Same as previous, but close up view. "Jackson's Big Hot Spring, Ashland, Ore." "The Land of a Thousand Healing Mineral Springs." 1920's. Shows a steam cloud on the right. In the 1860's Eugenia Jackson applied for water rights to the warm mineral water and artisan springs for "sanitarium and natatoriam purpose."

Pacific Highway near Jackson Hot Springs, 1920s. Road is paved.

Jackson Hot Springs, Ashland, Oregon

1960's view of Jackson Hot Springs, two miles S. of Ashland. "Located at the junction of U. S. Hwy 99 and Interstate 5; 50 x 100 ft. mineral pool, natural hot water, average temperature 72 to 88 degrees, health baths, trailer park, camping, modern cabins with electric kitchens, and color TV." Old Highway 99 crossed the present Pacific Highway behind Jackson Hot Springs (now called Well Springs).

Pacific Highway, Jackson County, Oregon. 1924 message reads: "The hills appear to be those lying just north from Ashland. Unhappy I can't send you a picture of the climate of Ashland, but let me say it's great and there can be no question, but you'll like it." Shows photographer's car and a white guard rail.

Postmarked 1916 from Medford. Message on back reads: "What do ya think of these fine country roads? However, this is a portion of the Pacific Highway." Road looks paved with a horse and wagon on the road.

Phoenix Motel, 4 miles South of Medford on US 99, Southern Oregon. 1950's view. Caption on back: New 21 clean units, thermostatically controlled electric heat and refrigeration, air conditioned, pool, 8 kitchenettes, ceramic tiled showers and tubs, TV available. Mountain view from some rooms. Quiet background. "Luxury and cleanliness that actually costs you less" readable on side of building. The town of Phoenix was laid out by Samuel Colver in 1854, and the post office was named Phoenix in 1857. Town originally named Gasburg.

Barkley's Tavern and Menagerie. "One of the scenic places of Southern Oregon, a rare collection of old guns and mounted animals from many countries. A handmade back bar of native black oak built in 1890." Highway 99 South, Phoenix, Oregon.

Colver House

Once the centerpiece landmark of Phoenix, Oregon, the Colver House was built in the 1850's by Sam and Huldah Colver; pioneers who rode the Oregon Trail to begin their life in the West. Constructed of logs fourteen inches thick, the house was one of the first built in the Rogue Valley. The home's location was on the main wagon road through the Valley and the Colvers always welcomed strangers, relatives, and friends into their home. Mr. Colver was a well-to-do, public spirited man who was often called "Uncle Sam." He willingly opened his home to be used as a community center; and the massive second floor as a schoolroom, dance hall, lodge, and church. In later years, this area was divided into thirteen rooms. The balcony spanning the front of the house was removed in 1918. In later decades, clapboards were added that concealed the original log walls. Sam died in 1891 at age seventy-seven; and Huldah, who loved her garden of lilacs and roses, died in 1907 at age eighty-four. Their grandson inherited the house and lived there until 1923 when it was sold and became The Blue Flower Lodge. After that, it was run as a dinner house; eventually becoming a museum and antique shop. In its final years the house was a private residence. Sadly, in 2008 it burned down under mysterious circumstances. One of the original logs was saved and put on display in the Phoenix museum.

ANTIQUES 1854 STAGE HOUSE - A Bit Of The Old West - Phoenix, Oregon

Late 1940's. Colver House - 1854 Stage House. A Bit of the Old West, Phoenix, Oregon. "The pioneer house built of squared logs, size 12 x 6 dovetailed together at corners and fastened with wooden pegs. Located on Highway 99 five miles South of Medford at Phoenix, Oregon."

Colver House 1950's view. "Gasburg Museum. Southern Oregon's hundred year old log house on Highway 99 at Phoenix, is now a museum of pioneer Americana." On the side of the building it says: GASBURG MUSEUM—OPEN.

"Modern Cabins at Evershady Auto Camp, 3 ½ miles South of Medford on Pacific Highway." 1930's. Shows small wood cabins with no garages.

"Free Auto Camp. Riviera Park on Rogue River, Jackson Co, Ore. F. C. Elliott Service Sta." Shows highway guard fence, pre-1920. "Fresh Buttermilk" sign. Shows store and gas.

1920's Riviera Park Auto Camp on Rogue River, Jackson Co., Ore. Shows a different angle of the same card as previous with a clearer view of the store. Sign reads: Groceries, Soda Fountain. F. C. Elliott Service Station. Also shows garage for general repairing. Another sign reads: Autos Stop Here.

Medford, Oregon

Medford is the seat of Jackson County and departure point for nearby Crater Lake National Park. The City is the gateway to the Shasta-Cascade Wonderland, which consists of Southern Oregon and Northern California along highways 97 and 99. The term "Shasta Cascade Wonderland" was penned because of good highways, good fishing, beautiful lakes and parks, lush forests, and Western history. It encompasses Oregon and California counties: Jackson, Klamath, Lake, Siskiyou, Modoc, Lassen, Shasta, Trinity, and Tehama.

Medford was established in 1883 by David Loring, a railroad right-of-way agent; but the City's name origin is unknown. In 1899 apple and pear seedlings were brought in by rail to thrive in Medford's rich adobe soil. The hearty abundance of crops led to Medford being the headquarters for several processing plants. Today, the nationally known Harry and David fruit processing plant is still one of the largest employers in Jackson County.

1940's aerial view Bear Creek Motel on U. S. 99, 1 ½ miles South of Medford, Oregon. (garage building on left side)

1930's Intersection corner of Riverside and Main Streets, Medford, Oregon. (Riverside was Highway 99). Sign above the street reads: MEDFORD THE GATEWAY TO CRATER LAKE. Merrick's Auto Camp sign is visible in the background.

"Looking West on Main Street from Highway 99 Intersection, Medford, Ore." 1940's. Central Avenue was Highway 99. Hotel Medford is in the distance. Hubbard's Hardware is on the right corner. Oregon US 99 shield sign shows arrows pointing straight ahead and to the right. Town signs on the right include: Portland, Crater Lake, Grants Pass, Eagle Point.

Looking South on Central Avenue from East Main Street, Medford, Ore. Shows Hotel Jackson and Central Drug.

"Big Y Super Market at Intersection of Pacific Highway and Camp White Highway, Medford, Oregon." 1940's. This building is still there as a grocery store.

"99" Motel. 826 N. Riverside, Medford, Oregon; Phone 2304. 1940's. The highway is in the foreground. Shows TEXACO gas station within the "99" Motel. Coke machine and rest room sign visible.

Medford TraveLodge, Medford, Oregon, 1950's. 722 N. Riverside Avenue.

Pulver's Motel, Medford, 1237 N. Riverside on Highway 99, Northbound. 30 modern units with telephone in every room and free radios. AAA approved.

MERRICK'S AUTO CAMP, MEDFORD, OREGON.   108341

Medford, Oregon, Merrick's Auto Camp. Postmarked 1928 from Medford. Message reads: " We are having a fine vacation. We are camping here for a few days. There are 75 cabins here." Merrick's was located at 112 N. Riverside Avenue. It was well known for its excellent accommodations offering cabins, cooking facilities, laundry, bowling, dancing in the ballroom, and swimming in the 50,000 gallon natatorium swimming pool. Bathing suits were rented to the ladies, and in winter the pool became an ice rink. In 1923 the city of Medford leased the management of Merrick's municipal auto camp, natatorium and inn. The Camp was located behind the Inn, and the two sites were connected by a bridge. Part of the camp was located on the other side of Bear Creek which paralleled Highway 99. Unfortunately, Bear Creek flooded in 1924 washing away several cabins. Merrick's closed in the 1950's.

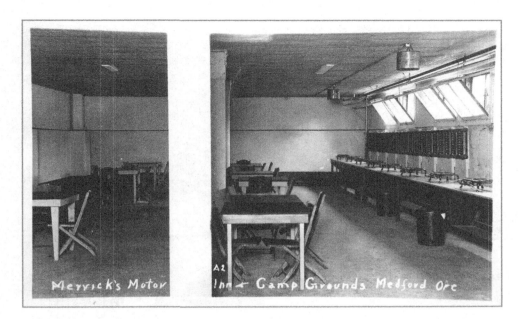

Postmarked 1924 from Medford. Captioned on front: Merrick's Motor Inn-Campground, Medford, Oregon. Shows gas stove tops on the right for cooking and dining tables and chairs. Sender writes: "This is some swell camp the best we have had." Sender also mentions taking a shower and going swimming.

1920 Merrick's Motor Inn, Medford, Oregon. Caption "In the center of a city of 15,000. Sixty-eight cottages have gas, running water, steam or stove heat, with or without toilets and showers, with or without linen; indoor heated plunge, filtered and chlorinated." Top view shows exterior, middle view shows the plunge, and bottom view shows the cabins.

Carole MacRobert Steele

Two ladies in front of a Medford auto camp … maybe Merrick's? 1930's

MOTOR HAVEN MOTEL
ON HIGHWAY 99
MEDFORD, OREGON

Motor Haven Motel on Highway 99, Medford, Oregon. Postmarked 1949 from Medford. Has garages, nicely landscaped, and lawn chairs.

Oakwood Motel, Medford, Oregon was located at 834 S. Pacific Highway. Caption: Units with kitchen facilities with electric ranges and electric refrigeration. Double coil box spring, inner spring mattresses. All units with garage. Large public lobby with fireplace. Fully modern with showers, gas heat.

Valley Motel, 3250 N. Pacific Highway US 99, Medford, Oregon. "New deluxe units. Tub-showers, free tv, kitchenettes." 1950's. Building still stands, but it's not a motel any more.

Carole MacRobert Steele

Phipps Auto Camp, Medford, Oregon. Caption: "On the Pacific Highway at Jackson Street. Free gas for cooking, free shelters, free showers. Thirty cabins, plenty of camping places. This is the ideal auto camp."

Hill Crest Orchard, Medford, Ore. The first fruit trees brought to the Rogue Valley were grown from seeds brought to Ashland. Apple orchards turned into pear orchards. Although this 1920's view is not on U. S. 99, it shows pear trees that were visible all over the Rogue Valley.

A Pictorial History of Highway 99: The Scenic Route   225

Native American buffalo roam "Blue Moon Ranch" Highway 99 Oregon. 1950's view show Table Rock Mt. on the left in the distance. This ranch was owned by John Stewart Day of Central Point, Oregon near Medford.

CHAPTER IX

Medford to Grants Pass

⊗⊗⊗

Table Rock Mountain

This four to five million year old mesa evolved after thousands of years of volcanic activity and erosion. Located at the northwest end of Bear Creek Valley between Medford and Gold Hill, this mesa, with its flat top and sheer walls, was a prominent landmark for traveling pioneers. There are actually two mesas ... lower Table Rock and Lower Table Rock rising 800 feet above the Valley floor. Lower Table Rock is downstream from the nearby Rogue River. The Table Rocks were the site of the Rogue River Indian Wars of 1855-56 when the white settlers attacked the Takelma Tribe living in the area and forced their relocation from Southern Oregon. In 1928 a marker was placed at the site of the Indian War. Each Spring 50,000 hikers climb the Tables Rocks to view the vernal pools that lay on top, along with seventy species of animals, three hundred forty species of plants, and two hundred species of wildflowers.

Table Rock from Pacific Highway at Tolo, Oregon and postmarked 1920 from Medford.
The town of Tolo was south of Sam's Valley near Blackwell Road which was part of
Highway 99. The road is dirt.

Table Mountain, Jackson County, Oregon on Pacific Highway, 1920's. Photographer's
car is shown passing through the orchards Jackson County's famous orchards.

Table Rock, Rogue River Valley 1920's. Road is paved. Photographer's car.

1950's Table Rock Mountain as seen from Highway 99 between Medford and Grants Pass. "In foreground is one of the hundreds of sawmills the traveler sees through Oregon." The familiar "Wigwam" burner is visible and was located to the east of Table Rock. They were a common sight along Highway 99 and throughout the Pacific Northwest. Almost every mill had one. Wigwams were conical-shaped with a domed mesh screen on top to prevent flyaway sparks. They were phased out in the 1970's and banned in the 1980's due to pollution. Most were torn down, but a few remain rusted and crumbling away.

For thousands of years Mt. Pitt, at 9,495 feet, served as a landmark to local Native Americans. Its name has a confusing history. As early as the 1830's it was called Mt. McLoughlin, after Oregon pioneer Dr. John McLoughlin, but it was also referred to as Mt. Pit. Often misspelled as Pitt, the name was derived from the Pit River in California; and some locals still refer to it as Mt. Pitt. In 1905 the Oregon Legislature officially named it Mt. McLoughlin.

Mt. Pitt from Pacific Highway 1920's Road is paved, but no center line.

Mt. Pitt from Pacific Highway near Central Point, Oregon, postmarked 1928 from Yreka. Message unedited: "Lost two hours at Roseburg to eat and have tire repaired. Stopped at Medford 1 hour so we hit winding roads over Siskiyou at dark arriving here (Yreka) at 8:50 so decided to go to bed early. It's now 6 a.m. And we'll leave in a few minutes. Expect to reach Oakland (Calif.) about 3 to 4 pm." That means it would have taken them ten hours to go from Yreka to the Bay Area ... a trip that today takes about five hours.

Mt. Pitt from Pacific Highway, postmarked 1937 from Medford. Road is paved with white center line.

Carole MacRobert Steele

Mt. McLoughlin, Southern Oregon. "Highway 99 in Southern Oregon between Grants Pass and Medford." Mt. McLoughlin in the background. Road is two lanes with yellow broken center line. Overpass visible in the distance. The 1950's station wagon is probably the photographers.

Oregon Interstate 5 "View looking South towards 9,495 ft. Mt. McLoughlin scenic Southern Oregon." Highway is now four lanes with center guard rail.

Gold Hill

The town of Gold Hill was founded in the 1850's when miners found a large gold nugget at nearby a hill site; thus, the name Gold Hill. $700,000 worth of gold was excavated from the mines that dotted the hillsides. When the railroad arrived in 1883, Gold Hill quickly developed into a bustling town. In 1895 the town was incorporated, and by 1915 it had two lumber planing mills, box factory, machine shop, and five gold mines with mills. The Ideal Cement plant was a major industry in town, but closed in 1968.

Gold Hill Bridge 1930's. This is the bridge that's crossed coming into town from the South on Pacific Highway. The railroad trestle bridge visible in background still stands. This is a Conde McCullough design open spandrel concrete arch bridge 442 ft. long.

Carole MacRobert Steele

Pacific Highway Bridge, Rogue River, Gold Hill, Oregon. Same bridge as previous, but different view. 1930's.

Gold Hill Bridge and Gold Hill town promotional 1940's card.

Rogue River Bridges, Gold Hill. Pre-1920's showing the railroad trestle bridge and the iron bridge; built before the concrete Gold Hill Bridge was built and shown in previous postcards.

Rock Point arch bridge near Gold Hill 1920's. Built at a cost of $48,000, it opened for traffic in 1920. Conde McCullough designed this bridge on the old Pacific Highway to conform and compliment the local rocky landscape. This was one of his first designs as a bridge engineer. The beautiful arched concrete deck with urn-shaped balusters and beveled handrails, replaced the 1899 timber truss covered bridge that once spanned the Rogue River at this site. Within a decade after being built, the bridge was already too narrow to handle the increased traffic; so its Northern approach was rebuilt in 1953. By the 1960's, Interstate 5 bypassed both the Gold Hill Bridge and the Rock Point Bridge. In recent years, $4 million was spent refurbishing Rock Point Bridge's cracked and damaged concrete deck and side rails. Thankfully the bridge was saved and not demolished!

A Pictorial History of Highway 99: The Scenic Route   237

Bridge over Rogue River, Pacific Highway (Rock Point Bridge). Postmarked 1924.

Pacific Highway over Rogue River near Gold Hill, Oregon, 1930's (Rock Point Bridge)

Carole MacRobert Steele

Rock Point stage station & telegraph office

Rock Point Stage Station and Telegraph Office; aka Rock Point Hotel on Highway 99 near Rock Point Bridge between Rogue River and Gold Hill. The town of Rock Point no longer exists, but in 1864 early settlers referred to the stage stop built there as "Point of Rocks." It provided an overnight place for people to stay while traveling between Sacramento and Portland. The hotel had thirty rooms, a bar, second floor ballroom, dining room, kitchen, and men's and women's parlors. The old Rock Point hotel at 40 N. River Road still stands. Since 1907 it has been home of the expansive Del Rio Winery. Located among lush rolling hills of vineyards, it's a popular tourist and wine-tasting destination.

Lazy Acres Motel on famous Rogue River, Gold Hill, Oregon. Caption: Lazy Acres Motel and Resort. 12 strictly modern units. All electric heating, cooking and refrigeration. On Highway 99. Reasonable rates … .Lazy Acres is now known as Lazy Acres Motel and RV Park with private beach and picnic area on the Rogue River at 2nd Avenue.

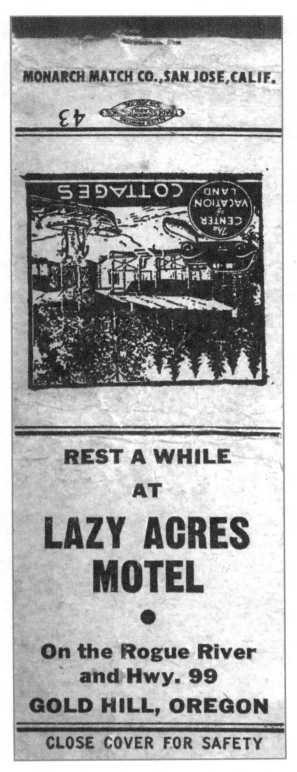

Lazy Acres matchbook "Rest Awhile at Lazy Acres Motel"

Lazy Acres, Gold Hill, Oregon 1940's.

Lazy Acres, Gold Hill, Oregon 1940's. Shows cottages with garages.

Edgewater Lodge, Highway 99, four miles N. of Gold Hill, Ore. Postmarked 1944. Caption: Modern cabins, cafe and lunch counter, service Station. Situated on the banks of the Rogue River. Good fishing, modern rates.

Gold Hill, Oregon. "The Deer Horns" Old Grandpa Lowe's; 1950's postcard. Deer horns mounted along the entire roof edge.

Close up of The Deer Horns.

The Gem Cottage, ten miles S. of Grants Pass, Oregon on US 99, 1940's. Sign reads: "The most beautiful stones in the world … agates, jaspers, opals. Jewelery and agate museum." Opened in 1940 as a business of cutting and polishing Oregon agates; custom jewelery and semi-precious stones. Building still stands on Highway 99 seven miles West of Gold Hill.

Carole MacRobert Steele

Old Oregon Historical Museum, Gold Hill, Oregon, 1950's. Part of a group of roadside attractions. Museum is now in the Belman-Martin House built in 1901 in downtown Gold Hill.

Rogue Riviera Restaurant. Four miles North of Gold Hill on Highway 99. "Take It In A Basket." Chicken noodles and hot biscuits. Building is still there and has housed several businesses over the decades.

Oregon Vortex and House of Mystery

Located at 4303 Sardine Creek Rd. on less than an acre, the Vortex is one of Oregon's oldest roadside attractions and world famous for its unexplained natural phenomena. The word "vortex" means a whirlpool of force which causes strange things to occur. In the 1890's the Grey Eagle Mining Company had a gold assay office at this site, but the gold never weighed correctly and the building was abandoned; later to be used as a tool shed. In 1907 during a violent storm, the small building slid thirty feet down the hill causing the ceiling, floor, and walls to be at steep angles. In the 1920's, John Litster, a geologist, mining engineer, and physicist acquired the property. He began to observe visual oddities in the building and on the property. Local natives already knew the area to be "forbidden ground" … a place to be avoided. Horses and other wildlife refused to go into the area, and birds would not nest in the trees. Litster and his wife were tireless promoters, so in 1930 they opened the "Crazy House of Sardine Creek" to the public as a tourist spot. In their brochure they advertised: "Nearby quartz mines may be visited and you can inspect gold-bearing ledges, tunnels, and shafts. The House of Mystery and old diggings are only 4 miles from Pacific Highway. Do something different! See something different! Owners of the property over the years have said that "whatever your education or profession, you will find a challenge to all your accepted theories." There is no explaining a broom that will stand by itself, or a ball that rolls uphill. The technical terminology defining this phenomenon is an "anti gravitational electromagnetic field. The Oregon State Department of Geology and Mineral Industries once claimed that it was merely an optical illusion or delusion. It's also been described as a "spherical field of force, half above ground and half below ground; by reason of this, the effected area is a circle." In 1959 the property owners claimed that, "it's strongest when the moon is full." The property is currently not for sale, but in 2003 the site and twenty-two acres was on the market for $3.5 million. It continues to be a highly popular tourist attraction and has been documented on TV channels such as: The History Channel, The Discovery Channel, The Learning Channel, and most recently, the "Ghost Adventures" crew made a visit.

The 165 foot Circle of "The House of Mystery", 1930's view shows the entrance with a twenty-five cent fee.

Oregon Vortex, Gold Hill, Oregon. 1950's view shows office and entrance sign: "All persons required to purchase tickets." Shows people ready for the tour sitting on a bench.

River Bridge—Rogue River, Oregon, 1950's. Message reads: "This is the bridge over Rogue River you come along 99 and then cross over this bridge. Then you are right up town." When the city of Rogue River was known as Woodville, the river was crossed by ferry. The bridge which replaced the ferry was built in 1909 and "made to stand forever;" however, in 1950 a new bridge was built. In 2006 a new cement span was built twenty-seven feet upstream from the old 1950 bridge … which was removed. The new bridge is currently referred to as the Depot Street Bridge.

Rogue River, Oregon. Lazy J Motel, ¼ mile South of bridge on 99. Postmarked 1953. "On the famous Rogue River between Medford and Grants Pass. Quiet, restful, deluxe

Carole MacRobert Steele

cabins. Kitchens with Frigidaire, fishing, swimming, hunting. Moderate rates. Owners Will and Georgia Jones. Message: "We did not make very good time driving today. They are working on the roads."

Scene on the Pacific Highway postmarked 1916. Somewhere along the Rogue River. A man on a horse and a man with a car. Logs used as guard rails and to keep the road stable. Very crude dirt road.

Pacific Highway on Rogue River, Oregon, 1920's. This view is between Medford and Grants Pass.

"Medford, Oregon on the World's Longest Paved Highway. Pacific Highway along the Rogue River" 1930's. The River is on the left.

Pacific Highway along Rogue River, Oregon 1930's. Road paved with white center line. River to the left.

Rogue River seen from U. S. Highway 99, Oregon, postmarked 1954. Paved road with white center line.

Savage Rapids Dam

Spanning the Rogue River, this diversion dam was built in 1917 by the Grants Pass Irrigation District to be used by farmers for irrigation purposes. It was named after the Savage family; early Grants Pass pioneers. In the 1950s, the dam was raised to hold back a greater amount of water, but as a result of the "water movement" in 2009 the Dam was removed enabling the River to flow freely from Lost Creek Dam to the Pacific Ocean. The remains of the Dam can still be seen from the highway.

Grants Pass, Oregon. Pre-1920 river road below Savage Rapids, Rogue River Valley.

Savage Rapids Dam. The highway following along the River is visible at the top of the photo.

Carole MacRobert Steele

Savage Rapids Irrigation Dam. "Water for 16,000 acres of rich land surrounding Grants Pass … Pears, apples, grapes, alfalfa; cheap land; settlers wanted. Grants Pass Chamber of Commerce."

CHAPTER X

Grants Pass, Oregon

Grants Pass owes its early existence to the Rogue River, mining and timber. When the Oregon Caves National Monument opened in 1909, Grants Pass became known as the "Gateway to the Oregon Caves". In the 1920's when roads and tourism improved, it became known as the "Gateway to the Redwood Empire" when the Redwood Highway was completed to the coast. The Rogue River has the greatest fly fishing in the world, and is the starting point for the famous Hells Canyon jet boat trips. In 1922, as the Oregon Caves fame grew, a group of Grants Pass businessmen formed the Oregon Cavemen booster club to promote the town's tourism. With their wild antics, they eventually became the most famous booster organization in Oregon and were internationally famous for of their animal skin clothing, wild wigs, fangs, clubs, and animal bones used as weapons. There are more than two dozen clubs and businesses with the word CAVEMAN in the name, as well as being the mascot for the high school.

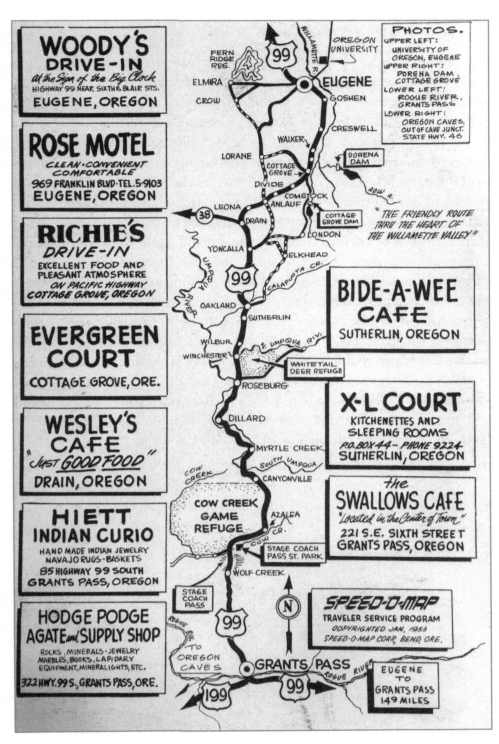

Speed-O-Map 1953 postcard with map of U. S. 99 showing all the towns from Grants Pass to Eugene, 149 miles. Advertises businesses along the way including in Grants Pass: The Swallows Cafe and the Hodge Podge Agate and Supply Shop.

Caveman Bridge—Grants Pass

The Caveman Bridge on 6th Street is on the National Registry of Historic Places and the landmark that Grants Pass identifies with. Dedicated in 1931, the Bridge takes its name from the local civic organization of the same name originating back to the opening of nearby Oregon Caves National Monument. This magnificent concrete arch is a Conde McCullough design. It boasts three 150 foot partial spans with lamp posts and railings inset with floral patterns. The bridge parallel to the Caveman also crosses the Rogue River and opened in 1960 to carry northbound traffic. With the fanfare of a parade and ribbon cutting, the Caveman Bridge was dedicated on May 23, 1931. The Governor in attendance as well as the Cavemen dressed in full regalia. In recent years, the decades-old bridge was in need of repair, and in 2019 it was rededicated after a $5 million renovation. Cracks needed filling, ironwork needed replacing; as well as new pavement and railings. The dingy gray color is now brighter with new resurfacing of the concrete and new lighting was installed. An Oregon Department of Transportation spokesman said of the bridge, "An irreplaceable structure; you couldn't build an exact replica with funds available today." Downstream from the Caveman Bridge was a wooden dam about five feet tall which provided a swimming hole for nearby Riverside Park. Sand was hauled in so the river bottom would be smooth, but it all washed away in the 1940's flood. The Rogue River flooded in 1927, 1955, 1964, and 1997.

Pacific Highway crosses the Rogue River at Grants Pass. This view shows the Robertson Bridge built in the early 1900's. This was a three-span steel truss style bridge. It was moved downstream to make room for the new Caveman Bridge, and still stands in that location today; but is closed to traffic.

Grants Pass Caveman Bridge dedication ceremony, 1931.

On the Rogue River, Grants Pass. 1930's.

Caveman Bridge on Rogue River, Pacific Highway, Grants Pass, 1930's.

Caveman Bridge spanning Rogue River, Grants Pass, Oregon. US 99 shield sign on the right. Motel and store roof visible on the right. 1940's.

Highway Junction #99 and #199, Grants Pass. 1940's view of entrance to Grants Pass via the Caveman Bridge. Visible on the right is Tracy's Steak House and Flower Basket Florist. Hidden in the trees is the Grants Pass Motel. Caveman Bridge in distance showing a 25 mph speed sign.

Tracy's Steak House … "Just Plain Better" … Grants Pass, Oregon. Breakfast, lunch, dinner, snacks, fountain. When new, it was a much smaller building.

1950's view of the Caveman Bridge showing the Riverside Motel. These two bridges; the graceful arched one in the background carrying southbound traffic, and the newer one in foreground carrying northbound traffic, span the Rogue River. Today this is 6th and 7th Streets.

Carole MacRobert Steele

It's The Climate Sign

In 1917, John Hampshire and his bride arrived in Grants Pass and found the area more heavenly than they ever imagined. With his occupation as a road builder, he soon became a Southern Oregon booster trying every way he could to entice travelers to the beauty and greatness of the area. With the slogan "It's the Climate" stuck in his head, he convinced six Grants Pass Commissioners to erect a lighted sign spanning 6th Street. On July 20, 1920 he paid $443.00 to have the sign hung, and it wasn't long before Grants Pass became known as the "Climate City." Over the decades the sign was moved several times. For a twenty year span of time, there was no sign at all, and the townspeople didn't seem to miss it. With the 1976 Bi-Centennial on the horizon, $5,000 was raised to bring back an exact replica of the original sign to be hung in a downtown location; and there is hangs today across 6th Street where thousands of cars pass under it everyday.

In addition to the Climate Sign, there was another sign on 6th Street in the early years that read: Register Cars Here. Motorists actually thought they had to stop and register, but the idea was to get tourists to stop so they'd leave some of their money. 6th Street was the "Main" street in Grants Pass. The North and South lanes of Highway 99 passed through the heart of town with its shops, cafes, auto parks, and gas stations.

Main Street, Grants Pass, 1920's. "It's The Climate" … "Out of State Cars Register Here." Main Street was the Pacific Highway.

Grants Pass, Oregon. US 99 shield sign pointing North and South directions. From Grants Pass to San Francisco was 420 miles South and Portland was 275 miles North.

Carole MacRobert Steele

Grants Pass Motels

River Shore Resort, 1940's … "By a Riffle On the Rogue." (a riffle is a rocky or shallow part of a stream/river with rough water). Address: 2126 Highway 99; two miles South of Grants Pass. Deluxe units, some with electric kitchens; cool and shady.

Cabins at Fred's Auto Camp, Grants Pass, 1930's. Cabins connected by open garages.

Fred's Place on Famous Rogue River, Grants Pass. 1940's. It now shows a cafe selling hamburgers, apple cider, renting cabins, and selling Mobil Gas. Cabins located d below these buildings with US 99 in front.

1950's Motel Del Rogue ... "Watch For Gus The Fisherman" (as seen in this photo.) Oregon US 99 shield sign on the far left. Address: 2150 S. Highway 99. Housekeeping cottages on the water's edge. Fishing, swimming, boating.

Rose Motel, 1 ½ miles South of Grants Pass on Highway 99, 1940's. Connecting cabins separated by open garages. Highway in foreground. Landscaped with patio furniture on lawn area.

It seems like every town in the Western United States had an El Rancho Motel, and Grants Pass was no different. 1.5 miles South of City on Highway 99, 1940's. Connected cabins with open garages. Highway in foreground.

Garden Plaza Motel, 1950's. On US 99 Southbound, 1 mile from Grants Pass. 21 air conditioned units, shady grounds. Room telephones, 24 hour heat, free radios, shower and tub baths. Some with kitchens, television lounge.

Weasku Inn ... Pronounced We Ask You

Clark Gable comes to mind when people mention Weasku Inn, located on Highway 99 between Gold Hill and Grants Pass. Gable stayed so often in the 1930's and 40's, locals thought he owned an interest in the Inn. He did own forty acres nearby, and had intended to build on the property, but he never did. He was once quoted as saying, "I'd rather be eating flapjacks at the Weasku Inn." It's rumored he spent weeks in an upstairs bedroom at the Inn mourning the loss of his wife, Carole Lombard, who died in the mid-1940's. Other celebrities such as Walt Disney, Zane Gray, and Bing Crosby vacationed at Weasku. The walls of the Lodge were soon covered with autographed pictures of notable people.

Alfred Smith opened Weasku Inn in the early 1920's. Smith felled trees on the property to build six bark cabins and a lodge. "We Ask U In" had a nice Indian sound, and by 1924, it had gained a reputation as a fine fishing resort. The cabins were furnished with a double bed, wood stove, and table and chairs; but you had to bring your own bedding and dishes.

The Rogue River was always the main draw, and in 1927, well-known fly fisherman, W. E. "Rainbow" Gibson and his wife, bought Weasku. Their movie star friends loved to come and stay. In the 1930's these new owners added twelve larger cabins with kitchenettes. There were six rooms on the second floor of the lodge which rented for $2.50 a night. The cabins rented for $3.50. In the mid-1930's a cafe was added. During Prohibition no alcohol was allowed at the Lodge; so guests sipped coffee while lounging in front of the huge stone fireplace in the living room.

In 1938 "Rainbow" Gibson died, and Peggy and their three daughters kept the Inn until 1958. In the 1980's the Inn fell on hard times and disrepair. In the 1990's the original cabins and the cafe were razed, and the nine acre property was put up for sale. It sat on the market for nine years. Luckily, by 1996 Weasku had been restored, reopened, and named "One of the 25 Great American Lodges" by Travel and Leisure Magazine. The original Lodge building remains, and Weasku Inn thrives despite the majority of traffic traveling on Interstate 5 … instead of Old 99.

Weasku Inn 1920's. "Lunch Goods" log cabin. Highway 99 in front.

BUNGALOWS
STRICTLY MODERN

SOUND PROOF
CONSTRUCTION

MOST COMFORTABLY
FURNISHED

Mr. & Mrs. S. C. Williams
Props.

NEW HOLLYWOOD COURT
On U.S. 99, ¼ Mile So. of Grants Pass, Oregon

New Hollywood Court on US 99, ¼ mile South of Grants Pass. Bungalows, strictly modern, sound proof construction, most comfortably furnished. Mr. and Mrs. S. C. Williams, prop.

Red Wing Auto Court, City Center, Grants Pass, OR. Postmarked 1931. Connected units with open garages; office in center.

Modern Cottages at Red Wing Auto Court. 1930's. Each cabin is numbered. On the far right is cabin #1.

Red Arrow Auto Camp, Grants Pass. Robertson Bridge visible on the right before the Caveman Bridge was built in 1931. Shows cabins along the Rogue River each with a red arrow painted on them.

Red Arrow Auto Camp. Shows cafe with "Eats" sign.

Grants Pass Auto Camp

In 1915 Grants Pass opened an attractive, comfortable and free auto campground called Riverside Best Camp in order "to make the stop of this class of tourists as pleasant as possible." Grants Pass was one of the first in Oregon to open an auto camp. Riverside Park had been established in 1914 and the City chose this site for the camp because the Park provided public access to the Rogue River. Built on the River's East bank, the Camp provided all the necessary conveniences to make the experience enjoyable. Grants Pass had always been a popular place for travelers who stayed in its hotels, but the City needed a municipal campground for auto travelers carrying camping equipment. It accommodated up to 5,200 autos during the summer months.

Beginning in 1923, the camp started charging fifty cents a night. In 1925 cabins with amenities were added to satisfy those wanting a more satisfactory overnight experience. As highway construction continued to improve, tourist traffic increased and soon the cabins morphed into the modern motel we know today with its higher level of comfort.

Riverside Auto Park, Grants Pass, 1930's. "Best Camp In or Near Grants Pass"

Riverside Auto Park, Grants Pass. 1930's sign reads: "The Best With or Without Toilets - $1.00 and up" "Cook with Gas or Electric" Two log entrances visible.

Riverside Motel (former auto park). Postmarked 1946 from Grants Pass. "At Caveman Bridge in City." Views show entrance, exterior with landscaping, and room interior.

Riverside Best Camp. (see previous postcard). 1930s. Knotty pine paneling and view of Rogue River and Caveman Bridge.

Riverside Motel Court. 1940's room interior with couch, double bed, dresser, two chairs, lamps, mirrors, and large floor radio.

Riverside Motel and Restaurant, 971 S. E. 6th Street. "Grants Pass' largest and most modern motel on banks of famous Rogue River. Air condition, sound proof, fire proof. Telephones, free television, private balconies, sundecks. Three blocks to downtown. Heated pool." Postmarked 1966. This motel sits between the Caveman Bridge on the left and 7th Street. The Bridge is on the right. Postmarked 1966. Now called The Lodge at Riverside.

Bridge Motel, 986 SW 6th Street, Grants Pass; North end of Caveman Bridge, 1960's. Hellgate excursions—scenic jet boat trips on the Rogue River exclusive at Bridge Motel. This motel is now called the Riverside Inn.

"Cottages at Camp Delight", Grants Pass, 1930's. Auto camp no doubt on Pacific Highway; but exact location unknown.

Grants Pass Auto Camp, Pacific Highway, 1930's. Exact location unknown. Attractive connected cottages with garages and landscaping; lawn and garden swings.

Grants Pass Auto Park (see previous card). 1930's showing a closer view of the cottages with cars in garages.

Cabins at Orchard Auto Camp, Grants Pass, 1930's. Exact location unknown, but is on the Pacific Highway. Two kids sit on bench.

Rogue Haven Motel, 943 SW 6th Street, Highway 99, Grants Pass. 1950s. Shows office and AAA sign on the left.

Empress Motel, Grants Pass, US 99, postmarked 1952. "Member Best Western Motels." Office is tall building in center section. Landscaped with Gladiola's. Canvas awnings over each window.

Wagon Wheel Motel, 1439 NE 6th Street. Older motel from the 1950's with garages between each unit. Lawn area with lawn chairs and wagon wheels.

Palm Motel in NE Grants Pass on US Highway 99, 1940's. Paved driveways. "Newest Court in Town."

Redwood Empire Sign

As highways and automobiles improved with each passing decade, more and more people wanted to see the wondrous sights California and Oregon; including the Rogue River along Highway 99 and the Coast Highway through the Redwoods. Grants Pass was at a junction where travelers could choose to take Highway 199 over to the California Coast and through Redwood National Park. The Redwood Empire Association promoted tourist travel for all towns from San Francisco to Grants Pass, and in 1941 they came up with a ploy to get people off Highway 99 and over to the coast via Highway 199. They erected a sign at the junction of Highway 99 and 199 at Caveman Bridge and 6th Street, directing traffic to the California coast. This original sign read: KEEP TO THE RIGHT FOR REDWOOD EMPIRE, OREGON CAVES, GOLDEN GATE BRIDGE, SAN FRANCISCO. The lettering was hand-painted and accented with neon lighting.

By 2011, after decades of service, the old sign was in need of restoration. Heated arguments sprang up about if and how it should be restored. It was showing different weathered shades of chipped green paint, the posts were rusted, and moss covered the face. The sign sits at its entrance of Riverside Inn. They own the sign. It's not an official State of Oregon sign. The townspeople

Carole MacRobert Steele

and Grants Pass City Council argued whether the sign was a historic landmark to be refurbished or replaced by a newer modern sign. Over the years there have been ten different renditions of the sign with wording changed.

In 2018 the Grants Pass City Council decided to tear down the sign, but there was such an impassioned outcry from the public, the City Council was forced to save the sign. The decision was made to restore, not replace, and $25,000 was set aside for the project. ES&A Sign and Awning Company of Eugene, Oregon was chosen to do the work. The aging sign was hauled away in pieces and transported to Eugene on a flatbed trailer.

In May, 2019 Grants Pass held a ceremony rededicating the beautiful new sign as it was unveiled to the public at its original location at Caveman Bridge. As cars pass by at night, the neon lettering shine brightly pointing the way to the Redwood Empire.

OREGON CAVEMAN - GRANTS PASS

Oregon Caveman—Grants Pass 1971. Message on back reads: "The nearby Oregon Caves National Monument has inspired people of Grants Pass to adopt the Caveman as its motif. This imposing statue greets the visitor as he approaches the City from the North." Erected to promote local business, this mascot has stood at the corner of NW 6th Street by the Chamber of Commerce building since 1971. In 2004 local vandals set fire to the statue. Local Caveman Club members and townspeople raised funds to have it repaired. As a result, it's now two hundred pounds heavier and flame resistant. It was proudly placed back on its pedestal in 2005 and has remained safe ever since.

Carole MacRobert Steele

1940's Redwood Empire sign. Redwood log with arrow pointing down Highway 199, which is the Redwood Highway. Words on the sign: "See All the Redwood Empire-- America's Newest National Playground Through 100 miles of Giant Redwood Trees to Diversified Vacation Attractions. Redwood Empire Assn." Shows Cavewoman dressed in animal skins standing by the sign.

Logging—Grants Pass, late 1930's. Mack trucks ... a common sight on Oregon highways.

Pacific Highway on Sexton Mountain north of Grants Pass. In the 1920's, the Sexton Mountain section of the Pacific Highway was well known for being tortuous, twisting, and turning. Even the improved thirteen foot roadbed with concrete curbs hadn't helped motorist to navigate safely. In 1944 a new alignment was completed. The Sexton summit was cut 100 feet deep and a mile in length; thus eliminating 132 curves that traversed the mountain. Six miles of the old road was abandoned and the new road regraded and repaved. Cars could now safely and easily drive fifty miles per hour.

Sexton Mountain from Pacific Highway, 1930's. Paved with white center line and guard rails.

Carole MacRobert Steele

CHAPTER XI

Grants Pass to Roseburg

Looking South on Sexton Pass, Highway 99, Oregon. 1950's. Four lanes with double solid center line. Grants Pass in the distance.

Pacific Highway near Grants Pass, 1920's. Road is paved.

Pacific Highway on Sexton Mt., Oregon. Photographer's car parked on the side, 1930's. Paved road with center line.

Near summit of Sexton Mt., postmarked 1928 from Roseburg. Message: "Did not go into Crater Lake. Will keep on towards Seattle. The folks are standing the ride ok."

Pacific Highway, Sexton Mt. Near Grants Pass. 1930's view. Road is now paved with center white line. Same view as previous card where road had no white line.

Carole MacRobert Steele

Sexton Pass looking North, Highway 99, Oregon. Late 1940's/early 1950's. Road paved with two lanes and white center line.

Oregon Stages scene on Pacific Highway, Sexton Mt., Oregon. Destination on bus is PORTLAND. Luggage rack on top. The Oregon Stages Pioneer Line began in 1927 over Sexton Mt. They were auto stages seating fifteen to twenty people which connected the Pacific Highway between Ashland and Portland.

Pacific Highway view from Sexton Mt. Near Grants Pass, 1920's. Paved road with guard rails; no center line.

Pacific Highway, Sexton Mt. Near Grants Pass, 1930's. Paved with solid white line.

Carole MacRobert Steele

Pacific Highway, Sexton Mt. Near Grants Pass, 1920's. Paved with no center line.

Pacific Highway, Sexton Mt. near Grants Pass, postmarked 1935 from Grants Pass. Part of message: "pending our vacation traveling through No. California and So. Oregon. The weather is beautiful and warm and the scenery unsurpassed."

Figure Eight—Sexton Mt. aka Grave Creek Loops and Double S; Sunny Valley. Message on back: "The road is so crooked, it is a figure eight." Located thirteen miles North of Grants Pass, the Sexton Loops were sharp and twisting hair pin curves that earned the name "Deadman's Curve". This original route required a Double S curve in order to come down the mountain into Sunny Valley.

The Double S curve, Pacific Hwy.

The Double S Curve. Sign on the building in foreground reads: RADIO PARK CAMP. This is a 1930's view showing the covered bridge in the background. Postmarked 1947. Radio Park in Sunny Valley was originally known as Carr's Corner for Cyrus Carr who purchased the property in 1922. In 1925 new owners renamed it RADIO PARK since they had the only radio in the area where locals could gather to hear the news. Radio Park boasted a grocery store, Texaco gas station, auto camp, and dance hall. The dance hall now houses the Applegate Trail Interpretive Center and Museum. In the late 1940's, Radio Park was renamed Sunny Valley.

A Pictorial History of Highway 99: The Scenic Route   291

Mt. Sexton Trading Post, Sunny Valley. Highway 99, sixteen miles North of Grants Pass. Redwoods Empire Info Service, cafe, groceries, gas, picnic area. This building eventually became Aunt Mary's Tavern (now boarded up) and was located where the highway comes down the North side of Sexton Mt.

Grave Creek Bridge

In 1846 the pioneers of the Applegate Wagon Train rested at Grave Creek before attempting to go over the tortuous mountains ahead of them. Martha Leland, a fourteen old member of the wagon train, died as a result of typhoid fever. Her pioneer family buried her body along the banks of the Creek beneath an oak tree on the present day roadway. Grave Creek Bridge got its name because it was Martha's grave site.

Grave Creek, at the base of Sexton Mountain, was a stage stop in the early days, and a popular stopping point along the Pacific Highway. Grave Creek Bridge was built in 1920 for $21,000 by the Oregon Department of Highways. This 105 ft. truss bridge is supported by "dumb bell" concrete piers. One of the few remaining covered bridges in Southern Oregon, it's also known as the Sunny Valley Covered Bridge. The Pacific Highway crossed this bridge, but it was completely bypassed when Interstate 5 opened in the 1960's.

In the late 1990's the bridge was closed to traffic for repairs to the approaches and bridge housing; reopening again in 2001. The Bridge is isolated on a strip of old bypassed highway, but it's drivable and offers some wonderful photo opportunities. Once across the bridge, the road ends leading to private property.

Grave Creek (covered) Bridge. Pacific Highway, 1940's.

Old Grave Creek Bridge on Pacific Highway, 1940's. Sign on left near fence reads: Grave Creek US 99. Oregon shield sign on the Bridge "Impaired Clearance". This view is looking back at Radio Park Camp and shows a Texaco gas station.

Oregon Stage Bus on Grave Creek, Pacific Highway, Oregon. Sign on the rear of bus reads: Oregon Stages System The Pioneer Line. In the background is the auto camp and covered bridge and shows the highway continuing up into the hills.

Pacific Highway on Smith Hill, Oregon, 1920's. The road is paved with no center line. Smith Hill was named after Henry Smith who came to Leland, Oregon in 1870. He took up land at nearby Wolf Creek in 1872; actually owning the land that Wolf Creek Tavern sits on. Smith Hill is also known as Wolf Creek Hill and is located on Sexton Mountain.

Loop on Smith Hill, Pacific Highway, 1930's. Paved with no center line.

Pacific Highway, Grave Creek Hill, Oregon. Lunch Room; eleven miles North from Hugo or Wolf Creek. 1920's view of Henry Dassey's "Mountain View Lunch Room" at the top of the hill near Marigold Auto Camp … a popular place to dance. Words on photographer's car spare tire says: "Oldsmobile Sets the Pace." Another sign that says FRESH EGGS and MILK.

Josephine and Douglas County Line. Wolf Creek Hill, Pacific Highway, Oregon. Sign by the 1920's car shows an arrow pointing to the right PACIFIC HWY. Tall white sign on the left says South Bound and North Bound Pacific Hwy with arrows. Same photographer's car as in previous Lunch Room photo.

1920's Pacific Highway near Wolf Creek. Paved road with white rail guard.

Oregon Stages System. Scene on Wolf Creek Hill, Oregon. Bus #44 bound for Portland. Luggage rack on top; no passengers visible.

Highway 99 near Wolf Creek, Oregon. 1940's two-way traffic, paved, widened, and white center lines. Shows two cars going North and two going South.

Wolf Creek Inn and Tavern

Twenty miles North of Grants Pass, nestled in a valley at the junction of Coyote and Wolf Creek, the Wolf Creek Inn was established in 1857. It boasts being the oldest continually operating Inn in the Pacific Northwest. Originally called the Six Bit House, it was built as a first-class stage stop for travelers coming from San Francisco to Portland; a place of comfort to spend the night and have a good meal. Builder Ben Holladay and his crew of local skilled craftsmen, constructed the Inn in 19th Century Classical Revival style with pillared front and an upper balcony. Holladay had several hostelries serving his stage lines, but when the railroad arrived, the Inn declined in popularity.

Through the decades it became known as one of the most lavishly furnished Inns on the West Coast; drawing such celebrities as Douglas Fairbanks and Mary Pickford, Clark Gable, and writer Jack London. It's rumored that London wrote his final chapter of "The Valley of The Moon" at Wolf Creek Inn. The Pacific Highway had reached Wolf Creek by 1922, and in 1925, a wing of eight additional rooms and baths were added for a total of twenty rooms. In the 1930's there was a semi-circular entrance to the Inn and a sign that read: Built 1857 Historical Wolf Creek Tavern. Famous fried chicken and steak dinners with homemade hot biscuits and honey 85 cents. Lodging single $1.00; double $1.50. With bath $2-$3. Breakfast, Lunch, Dinner 35 cents—85 cents.

In 1947 a realignment of Highway 99 bypassed downtown Wolf Creek, and in the 1960's, Interstate 5 bypassed the entire town. In the early 1970's a band of hippies stole many of the original furnishings from the Inn, but luckily in 1972 it was saved after being listed on the National Registry of Historical Places. In 1975 the Oregon State Parks bought the Inn and by 1979 the million dollar restoration was complete. The Wolf Creek Inn was open and ready to accept visitors and overnight guests. To maintain its historic atmosphere, it was furnished entirely in antiques with no TV's or phones are allowed in the rooms. The Inn remains a favorite for locals and tourists while serving excellent food and offering quaint overnight stays.

Entering Wolf Creek, Oregon showing Wolf Creek Tavern, general store, and garage. Tavern/Inn on the left, store on the right.

Historical Wolf Creek Tavern built 1857. This is a 1930's view. Dining room open 6 a.m. To 8 p.m. - Open to the Public. Pacific Hwy in the foreground.

Entrance sign says built in 1857—Historical Wolf Creek Tavern—meals, rooms, dining room open. modern hotel rooms—single $1.00, double $1.50. AAA sign and wicker rocking chairs on porch, early 1940's.

Postmarked 1952 shows lobby of Wolf Creek Inn. Detail shows Inn register stand near the staircase, mounted deer head, crank telephone near register, counter with cash register. Clock on the wall behind the counter reads 2:55; mail slots below clock. Standing ashtray by couch. Table and chairs with newspapers and magazines. Possibly a juke box in the back room. Staircase leading to upstairs rooms.

Wolf Creek store selling pure lard ten cents a pound, ice cream, and fresh meat. Gas with three pumps and garage next door selling Standard Oil products, 1930's.

1930's birdseye view of Wolf Creek showing the tavern with general store across the street and Standard Oil gas station. Auto camp to the far right.

Texaco gas station and auto camp at Wolf Creek, 1930s. Offers restrooms, store, and cabins renting for seventy-five cents a night. Cabins have open garages.

LAUREL AUTO CAMP
C. M. REED, PROP.
WOLF CREEK, OREGON

RECEIVED

RENT CABIN NO.

FOR CAMPING SPACE

MISCELLANEOUS

DATE

Laurel Auto Camp. C.M. Reed, proprietor, Wolf Creek. $1.50 to rent cabin. July 1928.

Carole MacRobert Steele

Capitol Auto Camp, Pacific Highway. This was located at Glendale, just North of Wolf Creek. Central building shows Union Gas station "non-detonating" cabins and camping. Cabins visible on the right. 1930's road paved with center white line and guard rails.

Cow Creek Bridge on Pacific Highway near Glendale, Oregon. Bridge constructed in 1919 using six wood pony trusses on concrete piers. Creosote and paint were used to protect the seventy foot structure. In 1913, Cow Creek had the longest descent down the steep mountain pass on a rough, rutted, and pot-holed muddy road. Large boulders projected up the sides of the road. The Cow Creek valley extends through ten miles of dense forest in a North and South direction.

"On Pacific Highway"

The Highway near Canyonville, Oregon.

Pacific Highway near Canyonville, 1920's paved road.

THE "SHASTA" IN COW CREEK CANON, OREGON

The "Shasta" in Cow Creek Canyon, Oregon. The "Shasta Limited" was a Southern Pacific train that started in 1895. It ran the Shasta Route through steep grades and sharp curves. By 1931 it was only running between Dunsmuir and Portland with service ending in 1938. It was replaced in 1949 by the "Shasta Daylight". This author rode the "Daylight" in 1954 when I was six years old. We caught the train in Oakland, California and rode it to Portland, Oregon to visit the relatives.

Carole MacRobert Steele

1920's scene near Canyonville (Cow Creek area), Douglas County. Paved road.

Pacific Highway, Douglas County, Canyon Creek. Narrow paved road.

Pacific Highway, Canyon Creek Canyon. Paved road with guard rail; no center line.

Pacific Highway, Canyon Creek, 1930's paved road with no center line.

Carole MacRobert Steele

Pacific Highway, Canyon Creek, Douglas County. 1920's paved road with no center line.

Pacific Highway near Canyonville. 1920's paved road with no center line.

458   PACIFIC HIGHWAY, OREGON

WINDING THROUGH PICTURESQUE CANYON CREEK

Winding through picturesque Canyon Creek, 1920's.

Canyon Creek Bridge

Built in the early 1920's, the Canyon Creek bridge was located six miles south of Canyonville. This twenty foot wide arched concrete structure was very important to the Pacific Highway serving as the main North-South route between the Willamette Valley in Oregon and the Sacramento Valley in California.

The Roseburg, Oregon chapter of the Daughters of the American Revolution placed a bronze plaque on the bridge that read: "Dedicated to the pioneers of Oregon, June 29, 1924. At the site of this bridge, the Oregon-California stage route travelers experienced the most arduous passage because of the rugged country crossed." In the 1950's the Pacific Highway was realigned through Canyon Creek and the bridge was demolished. As Interstate 5 was under construction, the Creek was altered, vegetation removed, and the Canyon sides were sheared to prevent landslides. The bridge and the DAR plaque are gone forever … .unless the plaque was removed beforehand??

1920's Pacific Highway, Canyonville; Canyon Creek Bridge; road is dirt. Message on back: "I am on my way to Crater Lake. We are going by car and camp along the way."

Pacific Highway on Canyon Creek a few miles South of Canyonville near Azalea. Shows the bridge in the distance as seen in previous views. This later view shows the road is paved with guardrails.

Carole MacRobert Steele

Highway 99 Douglas County, Oregon. Canyon Creek Bridge in distance. 1930's paved road with guard rails.

Canyon Pass, Pacific Highway. This card is dated 1934 on the back.

Carole MacRobert Steele

Canyonville in 1921.

"Canyonville 1921" Main Street businesses; road is dirt. Canyonville lies at the North end of Canyon Creek Canyon which opens into the valley of the South Umpqua River. The town developed along Canyon Creek because it was a stopping point on the route of the California-Oregon Stage. By the 1930's, five blocks of businesses on Main Street (Highway 99) in Canyonville were paved. The construction of Interstate 5 obliterated the Canyon and most of the earlier transportation routes. Old 99 remained, but the new highway bypassed the town.

Canyonville on Pacific Highway, 1920's busy Main Street with general store on the left.

Entering Canyonville. 1930's Main Street showing the general store, gas stations, and a cafe.

Downtown Canyonville, early 1950's. Rexall Drug building on the right and auto parts store across the street.

Carole MacRobert Steele

"Hello from Canyonville, Oregon."

1960's Main Street, Canyonville. Binders Department Store on the right; logging truck on the left with Canyon Mountain in the background.

Canyonville showing the Green Witch Tavern and Cafe and Gas. Sign on the building shows COACH SCHEDULE - Meals - 35 cent steaks.

Carrigan's Lodge, Canyonville, two miles South. 1930's paved highway.

At Alpine Lodge, formerly Carrigan's. Fishing pond in foreground. Alpine Lodge was located two miles South of Canyonville nestled in the deep canyon just off Highway 99. The original lodge built in 1932 was the home of Leander and Louella Converse

Carole MacRobert Steele

and their ten kids. The lodge offered lots of books to read by the fireplace on a rainy day while you listened to the radio. Cottages were built and a coffee shop was added. From 1935-1944 the owners had established a trout farm where visitors could catch their own mountain trout for dinner. There was a small lake for swimming near the cottages and a creek within twenty feet of the cottages. There were also duck, geese, deer, and pheasants on the property. The Lodge owners raised chickens and cows to supply food for their cafe. There were several owners through the years, and when the Lodge burned down, Interstate 5 took over the location.

Alpine Lodge, Canyonville. Late 1930's showing Union Oil gas station with three pumps. The main Lodge building to the left with highway in foreground.

Alpine Lodge Trout Aquarium. Late 1930's. Message on back: "Such a pretty auto camp and lodge." Sign on trout building says: RAINBOW TROUT FOR SALE. Lodge building in the background.

Alpine Lodge Coffee Shop and Motel, 1950's. Two Miles South of Canyonville on Highway 99. "Good food, modern cottages. We never close. Rest and relax in picturesque surroundings." Shows the original steeple roof cabins with open garages. Coffee shop in the background.

Carole MacRobert Steele

Canyon Auto Camp and Coffee Shop. 1930's log building promoted "cottages, dancing, plunge, garage."

Log Cabin Motel, Canyonville. Late 1930's-40s on Highway 99. New and modern. Serta mattresses. Ten cabins with or without kitchens, off the highway, quiet, restful. Floyd Harrington, prop.

Deer Park Inn. 23 miles South of Roseburg at Canyonville. 41 miles North of Grants Pass. Three deer grazing on the lawn. Located at 809 Canyon Creek Road, this home was built in 1898 for Mr. Stearns who owned it only a short time. Located four miles Southeast of Canyonville on old Highway 99, the house sat among dense native trees on a steep slope at the mouth of Bear Gulch. In 1914 or 1915, the Winn family bought the house to be used as a residence, but by 1920 they opened a portion of it to travelers. Mrs. Winn loved to sell her breads and pies to passing motorists. She planted a lot of shrubs which created a "park-like" setting where their pet deer liked to graze; therefore, DEER PARK became its name.

Umpqua River from Pacific Highway near Myrtle Creek, Oregon. Message on back reads: "It's so pretty along the Umpqua." 1920's paved road with center line.

Pacific Highway near Myrtle Creek, Oregon. 1920's paved road with white guard rails. Umpqua River on the left.

Scene on Pacific Highway at Myrtle Creek, postmarked 1926. Message reads: "This is the kind of country we go through up here in Oregon. It sure is a pretty place." Shows Umpqua River Bridge with earlier trestle bridge nearby. Railroad tracks in foreground. The arched concrete Myrtle Creek Bridge, also known as the South Umpqua River Bridge, was built in 1922 and designed by Conde McCullough. It was rehabilitated in 2007.

1920's Myrtle Creek Bridge. Road appears to be packed down, not paved.

1920's Myrtle Creek Bridge over Umpqua River.

Myrtle Creek Bridge and Pacific Highway, 1930's. Road is paved with no center line.

Myrtle Creek Bridge and Pacific Highway, 1940's. Now fully paved with center line and guard rail. A total of three Conde McCullough designed bridges spanned the South Umpqua River.

1923 Pacific Highway through Myrtle Creek, Oregon street scene. Known as "Gateway To The 100 Valleys of the Umpqua," Myrtle Creek was named for the groves of Myrtle trees that grew in the region when it was first discovered by settler James Weaver. The town was on the transportation route of the Applegate Trail and the stage and railroad lines. As automobile transportation increased, gas stations, repair shops, auto camps, and motels sprang up as seen in this photo. Most of the old highway between Canyonville and Myrtle Creeks lay beneath the pavement Interstate 5.

1950's Main Street Pacific Highway through Myrtle Creek. This view as you're coming into the town after cross the bridge.

Myrtle Grove Motel and Coffee Bar, Myrtle Creek, Oregon. This was six miles north of town in the 1950's. The large building is the coffee bar with gas pumps visible on far right.

Myrtle Grove Motel and Coffee Bar, Myrtle Creek, Oregon, 1950's. View of rustic cabins with no garages.

Myrtle Grove Motel, Gift Shop and Coffee Bar., postmarked 1956. Located on South Umpqua River. Twelve modern units, Beautyrest equipped, kitchenettes optional. Situated in grove of Myrtle trees. One of the principal rivers on the Oregon Coast, the Umpqua is one hundred eleven miles long emptying into the Pacific Ocean at Winchester Bay. World renown for fly fishing as well as salmon and sturgeon fishing.

Pacific Highway near Roseburg, 1920's crude road.

Same view as previous; postmarked 1926. Road appears to be paved. Message: "Tom met me at Ashland before noon yesterday. It was very hot and we drove on to a lovely old farm house in a big canyon 35 miles south of here (Roseburg). Very pretty country. We'll get to Portland about noon Monday." (she wrote this Sunday a.m.). The farmhouse she referred to could have been DEER PARK!

Same view as two previous, but this shows a close up of the two cement "bridges" visible in the other views. These are 1920's drainage ditch bridges.

Pacific Highway and Umpqua River, 1920's. Road appears well-packed or paved.

Carole MacRobert Steele

Pacific Highway and Umpqua River; crude road is 1920's.

Scene on Pacific Highway near Roseburg, 1930's. Road is now paved with railroad tracks next to the River.

Pacific Highway on Umpqua River. 1930's paved road with center white line and guard rail.

Umpqua River and Pacific Highway in Southern Oregon, four miles south of Dillard. 1930's paved road with center line.

Carole MacRobert Steele

Same views as earlier, but now shows Interstate 5 with four lanes and divider railing.

The Myrtle Tree

Distinctive gifts and serving pieces
from this rare wood featured at

Myrtlewood Treasure House

Winston, Ore.

7 miles S. of Roseburg on Highway 99

The Myrtle Tree. Myrtlewood Treasure House, Winston, Oregon, seven miles south of Roseburg on Highway 99. World's largest Myrtle trees on Highway 99, six miles north of Myrtle Creek. The rarest of all woods, Myrtle grows only in Southwest Oregon in Coos, Curry, and Douglas Counties. With its pungent small bay leaves, the tree goes by several other names including Pepperwood and Mountain Laurel. The coloring of the wood is unique with mulch-colored grains of red, yellow, and brown; some with many burls and shapes in the grain. It takes a century or more for Myrtles to grow to commercial size.

Carole MacRobert Steele

Myrtle trees growing along Pacific Highway near Roseburg. 1930's paved road with no center line.

"Among the Myrtle Tree" lining a State highway in Southwest Oregon. Valued by local craftsmen who manufacture many interesting and useful objects from it.

Adams Auto Park, Coos Junction seven miles south of Roseburg. 1930's individual cabins joined by open garages; lady sits in landscaped courtyard area.

Shady Oaks Motor Court, two miles south on Highway 99 business route, Roseburg, 1950's. This is a motel with connected rooms. It's still in business today!

South End Auto Camp, Roseburg, Oregon. 1930's little cabins with garages. The middle building is the service station with three gas pumps selling Violet Ray Gasoline. The other building is the office, lunchroom, and groceries.

South Umpqua River Bridge at Dillard, U.S. 99. Bridge built in 1939 by the Federal Works Agency.

South Umpqua River Bridge at Roseburg, 1940s. Shows the Oregon US 99 shield sign "South Umpqua River"

Roseburg

Located in the Umpqua Valley with the North branch of the Umpqua River winding through its foothills, Roseburg, Oregon is an unspoiled playground for hunting, fishing, golf, and boating. Aaron Rose, who platted the town in 1851, had opened a stable, tavern, store, and butcher shop. He called the town Deer Creek, but three years later it was officially platted as Roseburgh. The post office changed the spelling to Roseburg in 1894.

A 1936 travel guide described Roseburg has having "some of the best fruit and blackberries on the coast. Fertile valley, wide forests and clearings. Rich in grain and agriculture products. Abundant rain storms provide for storage reservoirs. Pleasing country with bright sunshine and a highly prosperous region."

Pacific Highway Entering Roseburg. River on the left. Train and tracks run alongside the River. Road appears to be paved, but no center line. 1920's.

1950's. Turn Around Inn at 1501 N. Stephens, Highway 99. Roseburg's original supper house and smorgasbord with chicken and steaks. Madge and Pop Davis opened it in 1946. The Baker's took over in 1947 and added a smorgasbord. Madge resumed control in 1948 concentrating on char-broiled steak dinners and fried chicken. A lounge was added in 1954. Located at 1023 N. E. Stephens Street and still standing.

Roseburg Greyhound bus depot, 835 S. E. Stephens. Late 1940's Art Deco style building still stands, but is vacant. Within the depot was Carl's Fine Foods Cafe. Highway 99 passed through the city center on Stephens Street. Replacing train travel, riding the bus became popular with those not owning a car. Pacific Greyhound Lines, founded in 1929, built a bus station in almost every city along US 99.

Hwy. 99 Business Route CITY CENTER MOTEL Roseburg, Oreg.

City Center Motel, 1321 S. E. Stephens on Highway 99 Business Route, Roseburg, 1950's. Described as AAA rated, beautifully decorated, tile baths, carpeted.

Rose-etta Lodge, 1067 N. E. Stephens St., Roseburg, Ore. 48 hotel rooms with ceramic baths, radios, telephones, free TV, radio, individual heat. In the heart of the timber industry and sportsman's paradise.

Hotel Umpqua, Roseburg on Pacific Highway 99; 1940s. Shows interior of coffee shop and lobby; J. A. Harding owner/manager. "Delightful stopping place for the traveler." (Before there were motels, travelers stayed in hotels located downtown)

ROSEBURG AUTO PARK, "IN THE HEART OF THE CITY." 50 MODERN CLEAN CABINS—50 TENT SPACE IN GROVE

1920's Roseburg Auto Park "In the Heart of the City." 50 modern clean cabins, 50 tent spaces in grove. 5 acres adjacent to Deer Creek North of Roseburg; lunchroom, service station. Claimed to be the first private auto park in Oregon. Still in business as of 1959.

Roseburg Auto Camp, 1930s. A later view from the previous postcard with many improvements.

BRAND'S—ON PACIFIC HIGHWAY 3 MILES NORTH OF ROSEBURG, ORE.   116410

Brand's on Pacific Highway three miles N. of Rosebrug, 1920s. "Famous lunching place, soda fountain, fruit market, and summer garden." "Eat barbecue sandwiches and live forever." Brand's was a roadside eatery and fruit stand since 1935. Chas. A Brand's specialty was barbecue. Handmade apple pie, ice cream, and milkshakes. In 1940 it doubled in size offering dinners and dancing.

Pool at Brand's three miles North of Roseburg, 1930s. Lady sits on cement bench watching lily pads float on the pond as water spouts up from the middle. Highway visible behind the lady.

CHAPTER XII

Roseburg to Eugene

Roseburg-Eugene Stage, Eugene, Oregon. "Safety Coach" on Pacific Highway.

Carole MacRobert Steele

Pacific Highway Eugene-Roseburg, Oregon. Late 1930's paved two-way road with center line.

A Pictorial History of Highway 99: The Scenic Route   343

Winchester Bridge, Pacific Highway, Douglas County over North Umpqua River. Also known as the Robert A. Booth Bridge, it was built in 1923 and designed by Conde McCullough. Named in honor of the Booth Family of Douglas County, it's located six miles North of Roseburg. At 884 feet, it was the longest bridge McCullough designed in the 1920's. Alcoves built for pedestrians to rest added to the charm of its Gothic Tudor architecture. The aging bridge underwent rehabilitation in 2008.

Booth Bridge on Pacific Highway, Winchester, Oregon. Opening day 1923 shows crowds of people walking across the bridge.

Pacific Highway over Umpqua River, 1930's.

Winchester Dam on Pacific Highway with Booth Bridge in foreground. Steel truss bridge visible behind the Dam waterfall.

C K 2375 - Booth Bridge, Umpqua River, Pacific Highway, Oregon.

1940's Booth Bridge, Umpqua River on Pacific Highway.

Dam at Winchester, Oregon, 1930's. Constructed in 1890, the Dam has been listed on the National Register of Historic Places since 1996. Originally four feet high, it was raised to sixteen feet in 1907, and was the main source of water and electricity for Roseburg until 1923. The hydro power facilities have long since been removed, and it's now kept solely for the recreational benefit of the Winchester Water Control District.

Winchester Dam, Roseburg, Oregon, 1950s. "View from the new bridge over the Umpqua showing the old bridge which is still being used." The "old bridge" referred to is the Booth built in 1923.

Winchester Dam, 1960s.

Sutherlin

Known as the "Gateway to the Oregon Coast," Fendel Sutherlin settled here in 1849 and developed his land for growing fruit. Called the "Father of Sutherland" in 1883, he was its wealthiest land owner, but it was his daughter who further developed the town. At the turn of the century the city of Sutherlin continued to push its development of the fruit and turkey industry, and by 1920 it had a population of five hundred fifteen. A 1990 issue of Oregon Business Magazine named Sutherlin as one of the fastest growing cities in Oregon.

Interstate 5 at Sutherlin, Oregon   Photo: Bernie McNeil

Interstate 5 at Sutherlin, Oregon. Interchange shows nearby gas stations and motels. 1960s-70s.

Sutherlin, Oregon, late 1950's. Four Winds Motel, US 99 freeway at Oregon Junction 225. Telephone Sutherlin 3821. 36 rooms, pool, TV, coffee shop, bowling alley, Union and Standard gasoline. Grand opening was July 18, 1959.

Sutherlin, Oregon. Built by Loring A. Wood. Date and words on building "1932 When Dreams Come True" Oregon Woods Camp. The largest log entrance of nature in the world. Taken from a dream. 100 feet long, 40 feet high, colored and lighted. Stop—It's Free—Look It Over." Loring Wood was a master model maker when he built his roadside museum and shop. He's shown standing in the doorway in this 1932 photo. Entrance into this museum was free, but later he charged twenty-five cents to view models of "Old Ironsides", the Mayflower, Golden Gate Bridge, and others he built. The building was constructed using 3,200 logs from 464 trees and was illuminated with colored lights at night. Its fate is unknown to this author.

Pacific Highway near Oakland, Oregon, 1920's. No center line.

Carole MacRobert Steele

On Pacific Highway approaching Oakland, Oregon, postmarked 1924. Highway is visible to the far right with railroad tracks beside it. Road appears to be graded dirt. Located on the Pacific Highway, but several miles from Interstate 5, Oakland was once the largest turkey shipping center on the Pacific Coast. The town was named for the groves of White Oak trees that dotted the valley. The town declined in the 1920s-30s, but luckily in 1979 many of its 1880's commercial and residential buildings were placed on the National Register of Historic Places.

Pacific Highway near Rice Hill, Oregon, 1920's. The summit of Rice Hill is 723 feet. The two mile long Rice Valley was named after William Street Rice who settled here in 1852. Today the town is a popular rest stop for truckers and motorists.

Pacific Highway, Rice Hill, Douglas County, Oregon, 1920's. Shows horseshoe curve.

Interstate 5 - Oregon - At Rice Hill　　　　　　　　　　　Photo: Morton Lu

Interstate 5, Oregon at Rice Hill. The A-frame roofs of the Ranch Motel are visible on the right. Also visible is the Ranch Restaurant and the Standard and Arco gas stations from the 1960's-70's. Now a PILOT truck stop, Rice Hill has long catered to motorists as a favorite place to stop for a burger and ice cream.

Close-up of the Ranch Motel at Rice Hill, 1960's. Captioned: Located at Rice Hill Exchange and Interstate 5; 25 miles North of Roseburg; 45 miles South of Eugene. Enjoy country atmosphere with TV, good food, and heated pool. (restaurant not visible)

Late 1960's, early 1970's Ranch Motel and Shopping Center. Captioned: 25 chalet-type units, TV, heated pool, restaurants, service stations, laundromat, beauty shop, gift shop. Rice Hill exit 148.

Pacific Highway near Drain, Oregon.

Carole MacRobert Steele

Pacific Highway entering Drain, Oregon, 1930's. Sign at other end of bridge reads CITY of DRAIN.

Road sign ENTERING DRAIN, Oregon. US 99 shield and billboards in the background.

Main Street scene, Drain, Oregon, 1950's. Shows hardware store, office supply store, drug store, and bank.

Totem Inn, Drain, Oregon, 1930's showing a cafe and Standard gas station. The Cafe also served as a depot for the Oregon Stages System. In 1935 this AAA approved cafe offered home cooked dinners for thirty-five cents; with salads as their specialty. The cafe and fountain were located on 3rd Avenue and B Street. It was remodeled several times after a fire in 1956.

Carole MacRobert Steele

Drain, Oregon, El Camino Motel. Caption: "On Highway ninety-nine. Beauty Rests, electric heat, showers in line. In a fast growing town called Drain where most folks are jolly, shine or rain; restful, quiet like a country lane." Late 1930s early 40s. Shows open garages. Located at 5355 Cedar Street, the El Camino opened in 1950 with twenty units, electric heat, showers. Drain had been a booming town until 1955 when the Highway 99 realignment closed Drain off from the rest of the traveling population. The gas station remained and the auto court was turned into apartments.

El Camino Motel, late 1950's. Shows the Carlsons; motel owners. Located two miles South of Yoncalla. The garages appear to be gone.

A Pictorial History of Highway 99: The Scenic Route   357

Late 1940's Yoncalla Main Street. Stores include: Yoncalla Drug, Krem's Market, tavern, and real estate office. No center line on street. Established in 1851 with Jesse Applegate as first postmaster.

Pacific Highway in Pass Creek Canyon, 1930's near Drain, Curtin, and Anlauf in Douglas County. Road paved with white guard rails. (Pass Creek through Curtin was destroyed when Interstate 5 was constructed in the 1960's).

Carole MacRobert Steele

ANLAUF-ELKHORN AUTO PARK   C-330

Anlauf-Elkhorn Lodge at Anlauf, Oregon between Drain and Cottage Grove, 1930's. Owners, Mr. and Mrs. W. C. DeLacy. Shows the Lodge with dining room and three gas pumps in front and a CABINS sign. Anlauf started out in the early 1920's as an auto campground eleven miles south of Drain. Eleven cabins, a store, service station, and ice cream soda fountain were constructed. Anlauf was on the line of the Southern Pacific Railroad and named after pioneer family Frank Anlauf and son Robert. In the 1950's it was known as the Anlauf Motor Lodge, but fire destroyed it in 1960.

Anlauf-Elkhorn, Oregon. A later view than previous one. Now shows big UNION ASSOC. GASOLINE and SHELL signs. Log cabins on the right renting for $1.00 a night.

At Anlauf-Elkhorn, 1930's. Two log cabins with open garages.

Cottage Grove

In 1855 G. C. Pearce was the first postmaster. His home was in a small grove of oaks, and he named the town as a reflection of his dwelling ... Cottage Grove! Cottage Grove sits in the heart of the world's largest stand of Douglas Fir trees. Lane and Douglas Counties contain more lumber than any other State except Oregon, Washington, Idaho, and California. By 1915 there were twenty-five lumber mills; but by the 1970's the mills were in decline. Cottage Grove has been the location of a couple of movies. In 1926 Buster Keaton filmed a Civil War comedy here called "The General." In 1977 National Lampoon's "Animal House" with John Belushi had a famous parade scene in downtown Cottage Grove. At one point, when the Pacific Highway was realigned through Cottage Grove, the highway was rerouted up 5th Street to Main Street.

Cottage Grove Main Street about 1915.

Cottage Grove with McCoy's Pharmacy prominent on the corner. Same view as previous, but fifty years later!

Cottage Grove, 1960's-70's view of the Village Green; a resort business hotel with a pitch-n-putt golf course, bowling alleys, gift shop, children's playground, and heated pool. Highway 99 visible at the top near Flying A gas station.

Pierce Barn—Cottage Grove

Dr. Ray Vaughn Pierce (1840–1914) was in the business of selling questionable "miracle cures" in the late 1800's and early 1900's. He liked to advertise his medicines by painting signs on barns all over the United States. In 1912 Dr. Pierce decided he wanted to use a barn belonging to Cottage Grove pioneer John Cochran, and Cochran agreed to the signage being painted on his barn.

In 1989 the current landowner threatened demolition of the barn; much to the consternation of locals. The Cottage Grove Historical Society banded together to try and save it, but by 2011, they had to abandon their efforts to purchase the barn. The owner claimed the barn was unsafe and wanted to sell the barn, house, and acreage for $285,000; more than the Historical Society could raise. In 2012 the barn owner was not completely unsympathetic to the value of local history and decided to take down the signage on the barn board-by-board; numbering and saving each with the idea of selling them for $25,000. Needless to say, the iconic barn is no longer standing.

COTTAGE GROVE LANDMARK

Cottage Grove Landmark. Card caption: Standing by the Pacific Highway, this old painted barn has caught the attention of passers by since 1919." I don't know if that 1919 date is correct since Dr. Pierce died in 1914. This drawing was done in 1987 by artist Roger Lovelace who died in Cottage Grove in 1990. Words on the barn: "For Your Liver—Dr. Pierce's Pleasant Pellets"

Cottage Grove. Landon's Motor Lodge and Restaurant, late 1940's. Highway with center line in front.

Willamette Valley and Willamette River

The Willamette Valley is one hundred fifty miles long with the Willamette River flowing the entire length of the Valley; surrounded by the Cascade Range, Oregon Coast Range and the Calapooya Mountains. Described as the "promised land of milk and honey," the emigrants who traveled the Oregon Trail wanted to settle in this agriculturally rich land. Providing water to the settlers was the Willamette River, a major tributary of the great Columbia River. The Willamette Valley has eight of Oregon's ten largest cities, which equals seventy percent of Oregon's population. Today, the Valley is known as "wine country" with its reputation for award winning wines.

Pacific Highway entering Willamette Valley, 1930's. Shows three cars on the highway with a white guard rail.

Pacific Highway, Lane County, postmarked 1924 from Siskiyou, Oregon. White guard rail with railroad tracks on the right.

PACIFIC HIGHWAY, ALONG THE WILLAMETTE RIVER NEAR EUGENE, OREGON. 107901

Pacific Highway along Willamette River near Eugene, 1920s. The road runs by the River with white guard rails; railroad tracks in foreground.

456. PACIFIC HIGHWAY, OREGON.

ALONG THE WILLAMETTE RIVER. 107818

Pacific Highway along Willamette River near Eugene, 1920's. Road is dirt with rock guard wall.

CHAPTER XIII

Eugene to Salem

Eugene

Located on the Willamette River, Eugene was named after its first settler, Eugene F. Skinner. Situated at the South end of the Willamette Valley, the City is a starting point of many scenic trips throughout this part of the State. Well known as the home of the University of Oregon, Eugene is also famous as the birthplace of NIKE; the world famous sports gear company. Eugene was the first city in Oregon to have one-way streets!

Looking East from Judkins Point, Eugene, Ore, 1940's. Willamette River on the left. Franklin Blvd (Hwy 99) crosses the Willamette River with Judkins Point rising to the left.

Eugene … Franklin Blvd … Highway 99 looking West from Judkin's Point. Entry into Eugene from the South. 1950's showing two-way traffic with four lanes.

Seaver's Eugene Auto Camp, two miles South of Eugene, Oregon. 1928 newspaper article described Seaver's Camp as being located at the junction of McKenzie and Pacific Highways; open day and night. Twenty-seven cottages; $1 - $1.50 per day with wood heat, gas to cook with, and water in the kitchen. The Camp had a laundry, hot shower baths, groceries, restaurant, service station. "The most modern Camp at Eugene."

Carole MacRobert Steele

Eugene, Oregon Tourists Auto Camp, postmarked 1922. Each car is parked at their own spot with pitched tens or tent canopies attached to the car. It appears that each assigned spot has a wooden table. Office building or shower/bathroom building is in the background. Road is foreground is dirt.

Eugene, Oregon. Holly Motel, 6036 Pacific Highway South, 1950's. Motel has open garages, offers TV. Highway in foreground.

Eugene, Oregon; Oak Court, Highway 99 N, 1930's. Has open garages; office building in front. Landscaped with lawn area and chairs.

Eugene; The Broadway Motel, 659 E. Broadway, South Highway 99. Walking distance to University of Oregon campus. Restaurant close by, connected rooms. 1950's.

Carole MacRobert Steele

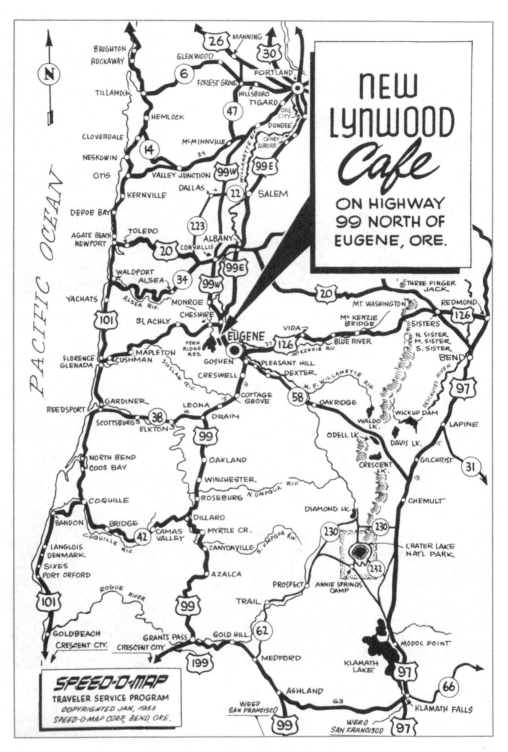

Shows all of the towns on 99 from Ashland the Portland.

Early 1950's. Harold and Effie's New Lynwood Cafe, Coffee Shop, and Dining Room. Highway 99 North of Eugene.

Eugene, Oregon. FORDS Drive Inn Coffee Shop, 1769 Franklin Blvd. Across from University of Oregon campus. Site of the first drive-in restaurant in Oregon. Serves ten thousand guests weekly; car hop service.

Springfield, Oregon, 1940's. Bridge across the Willamette River built in 1929 and designed by Conde McCullough; also known as the Willamette River Bridge.

Pacific Highway of Lane and Benton County, Linn, Oregon, 1920's. Shows photographer's car and the road is compacted dirt.

Junction City

Junction City, Oregon was settled early in the century mostly by Danish families. In 1961 the city held a Scandinavian Festival. Located in Lane County, Junction City is where 99W and 99E merge into 99. In 1871 the town received its name from an unfulfilled anticipation of a junction of two railroad lines; the Oregon/ California Railroad junction point that never happened. The town was successful in its development as a major shipping center for agricultural products grown in the region. In the 1910's-20's, the Pacific Highway put Junction City on the main road continuing North to Albany and Portland; however, in the 1930's, an alternate route was constructed from Junction City. This split road was officially titled US 99N and US 99E. Junction City is miles away from Interstate 5, but the Old Highway 99's are still heavily traveled going North.

Junction City, Oregon Main Street, postmarked 1939 from there. Message reads: "Staying at Junction Hotel. Have a good boarding house." Shows Brown Bros. Drug store with City Market across the street.

Junction City, 1950's Main Street, Highway 99. On the left is a SHELL gas station with Dairy Queen next door. Richfield and Texaco down the street. Chevrolet dealer on the right.

Junction City, 1960's. City Center Motel on US 99, South of Junction 99W. Some apartments for families.

Corvallis, Oregon. Wa-Wona Court, postmarked 1937 from there. It was located at 816 S. Third … aka Highway 99. Cute cottages with open garages. Message on back: "This was our home last night. Have been riding in the rain for two days. This country is beautiful if it does rain all the time." Corvallis is located on US 99 West; far from Interstate 5. Home of Oregon State College.

Tangent, Ore. five miles South of Albany. One mile N. of Tangent. Deer Lodge Motel. Cement deer statue on exhibit under motel sign. Connected cottages with nice landscaping, 1940's.

1943.

1943 snapshot of lady posed by Oregon U. S. 99E shield sign; Albany, Oregon.

Albany

In 1848 the City was named after New York's state capitol at Albany. Highway 99 passes through North Albany on Salem Avenue which becomes Old Salem Road. There are three historic districts in Albany that are on the National Register of Historic Places.

Albany, Oregon, Allen's Camp on US 99E; postmarked 1935 from there. Shows gas pumps in front with cabins around and behind the main building where owners lived. Allen's Camp was founded by brothers Dodge and Neil Allen in the 1930's. Located at 1415 Salem Road, there was a service station, grocery story, and a row of fourteen cabins to serve the traveling public. Rent was $1.25 to $2.50 a night. In 1936 Allen's became Woodland Square Apartments and was demolished in 2007.

Albany, Or. City Center Motel at the Junction of 99E and Highway 20; 1950s. Connected rooms with open garages. Offered TV, but the buildings are vintage 1930s'40s.

Carole MacRobert Steele

1953 Exterior and interior of the Red Hat Restaurant on Highway 99E.

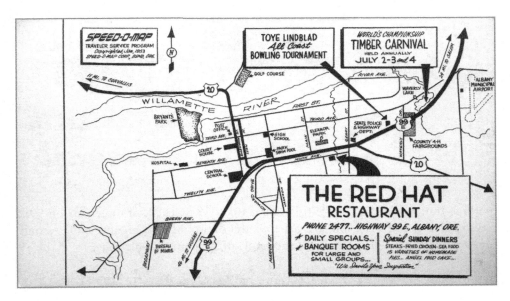

Albany, Oregon

CHAPTER XIV

Salem

THE PINE INN

4570 Portland Rd. - 1½ Miles North of Underpass on 99E - Salem, Ore.

The Pine Inn; Salem, Or. At 4570 Portland Rd, 1 ½ miles N. of underpass on 99E. Served chicken and steak dinners. Salem is the capitol of Oregon and is the second largest city on the Willamette River and home of Willamette University.

Salem, Or. 1950's Wooroffe's San-Shop.

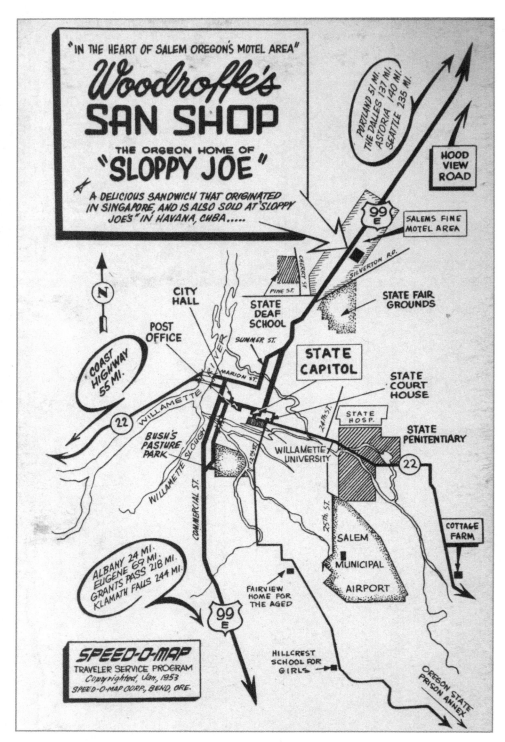

"In the heart of Salem's Motel Area." Oregon home of "Sloppy Joe." Offered car hop service featuring eighty-five cent king size hamburgers, salads, pies, ice cream, and five cent malts.

North Salem Motel Auto Court; ultra modern cottages. 2673 N. Pacific Highway 99E. 1930's with steam heat, tile baths, innerspring mattresses, and paved driveway.

Salem, OR. Rose Gardens Motel; 3350 Portland Rd., US 99E. Postmarked 1949 with message on back: "Roses are blooming all over this State; bloom the year round. In fact we have a rose garden next to our cottage." Twenty new rooms and apartments, electric heat. The the 1950's-60's the office was remodeled, and their caption read: "spacious grounds with rose gardens featuring 25 varieties; 22 units, 6 with kitchens; myrtlewood furniture, garages, off highway."

The Gables—Salem's Finest Auto Court near City center on Highway 99E; South Commercial Street. 1940's connected units with open garages.

LaVista Court on Highway 99E. South Salem limits located at 2990 Commercial Street SE. By the 1960's it had a pool where the motel sign is; had garages. Motel is gone and the land now a strip mall.

Carole MacRobert Steele

1960's Nopp's Golden Pheasant, 248 Liberty Street NE Salem on Highway 99E. Homemade rolls and pastries. All electric kitchen in full view of customer. Lunch 90 Cents - $1.35; dinners $1.10 - $3.15.

580. FARM SCENES, PACIFIC HIGHWAY NEAR SALEM, OREGON.   112716

Pacific Highway near Salem farm scene. 1920's road is paved.

1920's peaceful scene on the Pacific Highway .

Carole MacRobert Steele

CHAPTER XV

Salem to Portland

⋙✦⋘

THROUGH THE PINES, NEAR SALEM

Through the pines near Salem, 1920's. Road is paved with white center line and guard rails.

Salem, Oregon Blossom Day; acres of fruit trees in full bloom as seen from the highway.

Pacific Highway South of Salem, late 1930's. Two-way paved road with fruit trees on the hillsides.

Carole MacRobert Steele

MARION-POLK INTER CO BRIDGE OVER WILLAMETTE RIVER, OPENED 7-30-1918, SALEM ORE,

Marion-Polk Inter County Bridge over Willamette River, Salem, Oregon; also known as Center Street Bridge. The bridge was dedicated on July 30, 1918 "in a burst of patriotic fervor" with twenty thousand in attendance viewing the parade. To pay for the festivities, $3,000 was raised by various concessions selling post-cards, lunches etc. A man paid $500.00 to be the first to drive over the bridge in a FORDSON tractor, and a woman paid $100.00 to be the first to turn on the lights illuminating the bridge. In this view, American flags are visible on each side indicating this was probably Dedication Day. The approaches were replaced in 1953, and in 1983, the main span replaced the old one.

Brooks, Oregon; Buffalo Cafe and Curios, Highway 99E, twelve miles North of Salem. Oregon's only cafe and antique shop with a life size buffalo statue; sculpted by Everett Sloan of Salem. Hosts Harry and Vivian Barrick, 1960's.

Woodburn

The town was platted in 1887 by A. J. Settlemeir. The railroad right-of-way went through a large grove of trees that surrounded his cleared fields. One winter a fire got out of control burning trees and brush along the tracks, and that's how Woodburn got its name. The Settlemeier house still stands today as a museum. In 1923 a sign was erected across the Pacific Highway "World's Berry Center." When the road was widened the sign was removed; not only because it was damaged, but it presented a hazard because of increased highway traffic.

Woodburn, Oregon 1923 entrance sign "World's Berry Center." Road is paved and card postmarked from Woodburn 1925.

Woodburn, Oregon, late 1940's Main Street. Shows depot with railroad tracks on the left. All businesses are on the right side of the street.

Woodburn, Oregon, Highway 99; 1940's businesses, including a Union Oil gas station on the right. Across the street is the Pacific Motel and Cottages with Chevron Gas next door. Four lanes with two-way traffic.

Hubbard, Oregon roadside attraction on Highway 99E, south of Portland, twenty-two miles north of Salem ... ZOO AUTO PARK; Cabins, sandwiches, fountain service, Standard Gas, Goodyear tires. "Stop and See Wild Animals." The Loney family owned the auto park and zoo in Hubbard in the 1930's. Before them, it was owned by the Ames'. The train went by a block away and could be seen from the store benches at the auto park. Three to four hundred "bums" rode the train during the Depression.

The story goes that Mr. Loney asked them if they wanted some work. Some of these men had been loggers, and Mr. Loney asked them if they'd cut his five acres of trees in return for clothes, shoes, food, and shelter for five days. When the job was done, they were each given $2.00, two packages of cigarettes, and a packed lunch.

ZOO AUTO PARK ON PACIFIC HIGHWAY NEAR HUBBARD, OREGON

Zoo Auto Park on Pacific Highway one mile north of Hubbard, Oregon. This is a 1930's view in which Stanley and Margaret Loney wrote a message on the back of this postcard: "This is the park where we live. All the cabins are down under the trees. The little white buildings are the animal cages." By 1947, Robert and Dixie Brandt owned the auto park/zoo.

A quiet ride at McMinnville, Oregon"On the Road of a Thousand Wonders." This pre-1920's dirt road view is above Salem near Woodburn and Hubbard. McMinnville was known as "The Walnut City and Home of Linfield College." Located in the heart of the Willamette Valley, it had food processing plants, saw mills, and turkey farms.

Welcome to Newberg, Oregon, 1922. Both pedestals say "Newberg" and "Welcome." Each has light globes on top, and the road is paved with two-way traffic.

Oregon City

In 1842 Oregon City was the first seat of government for the Oregon Territory. Settled in 1829-30 on the Willamette River, it was the first incorporated city West of the Rockies. Known as a city with heavy industry, the Willamette Falls drop forty-two feet to generate electric power. Factories were built on bedrock foundations. The Pacific Highway was chiseled out of rock bluffs on the East bank of the Willamette River at an elevation enough to gain entrance and exit to the City.

The Super Highway near Oregon City shows 1940's four-lane paved road with center lines. The little building on left side of road says: CABINS~EGGS LAID TODAY.

Pacific Highway from the New Era Hill which was located on 99E between Oregon City and Canby in Clackamas County. Once a thriving spiritual camp and agricultural community, it's now a semi-ghost town. The post office existed from 1876 to 1940.

Oregon City and Pacific Highway bluffs; 1920's paved road.

Carole MacRobert Steele

Highway 99 and paper mills at Oregon City, 1940's four lanes paved. City elevator visible in the background. Hawley Pulp and Paper Company on the left.

Pacific Highway and paper mills at Oregon City; late 1930's early 1940's.

Oregon City Bridge

The steel arch bridge crosses the Willamette River from Oregon City to West Linn. Built in 1922 by Conde McCullough, it was placed on the National Register of Historic Places in 2005 and is owned by Oregon Department of Transportation as part of Route 43. Located downstream from the Willamette Falls and Willamette Falls Locks. It was built to replace the 1888 pedestrian suspension bridge which was demolished when the new bridge was built at a cost of $300,000. The piers originally had public restrooms, but they were closed in 1937 due to vandalism. In 2010-2012, the bridge had extensive rehabilitation at a cost of $15 million. It's the only bridge in Oregon to be encased in granite to protect it from emissions of the nearby paper mills, and no longer are commercial vehicles weighing more than fourteen tons allowed to cross the bridge.

Pacific Highway through Oregon City. Arch Bridge over Willamette River. 1940's view shows the highway winding around the downtown area.

Pacific Highway through Oregon City approaching the arch bridge; 1940's.

Pacific Highway Bridge over Willamette River at Oregon City; 1940's.

Oregon City Elevator

Oregon City is formed on two levels. The first level is a narrow strip a few blocks wide wedged between the Willamette River and a ninety foot basalt cliff. The second level sits on top of a cliff. At the turn of the century a slippery path was used for foot traffic to traverse the two levels. Wooden stairs were built, but not providing much improvement. In 1912 voters elected to have a 130 foot municipal water-powered elevator built that would take them between the two city levels. Completed in 1915, the elevator was powered using 200,000 gallons of water each day taking three minutes to rise from the bottom to the top. By 1924 the elevator ran on electricity and took thirty seconds from bottom to top. In 1952, $175,000 was raised to replace the old elevator and an observation deck was built with views of Willamette Falls and Locks. Today the ride only takes fifteen seconds and is still being used today to lift pedestrians ninety feet from the business area to the lower residential level. It's the only "vertical street" and outdoor elevator in the United States.

Oregon City Elevator with arch bridge to the left; 1940's. Message on back: "The little town across the bridge is more like part of Oregon City, but it's called West Linn."

Oregon … City Gene and Joe's Restaurant, 19000 S. E. McLoughlin Blvd. US 99E; 1950's … ¼ lb. broiled hamburgers. Shows a lady dishing up hamburger fixings while the lady on the right is at the salad bar, and the chef flips burgers.

Willamette Falls

Willamette Falls is a horseshoe-shaped waterfall caused by a basalt shelf in the river bottom. The Falls are forty-two feet high and fifteen hundred feet wide; the largest by volume in the Northwest. The Willamette Locks are located around the Falls, and are the oldest continually operating multi-lift lock and canal system in the United States. There is a view point on Highway 99E which offers a closer looks at the Falls, bluffs, and scenery. For a history of the Falls, a museum housed in the old Lock master's office offers self-guided tours. From this location, it's a perfect vantage point to watch boats passing through the lock system.

Oregon City … Willamette Falls located on McLoughlin Blvd. aka Old 99E. Message on back: "When river rises the falls are covered up, but two large paper mills get their power from these falls."

Clackamas Bridge super highway between Oregon City and Portland over the Clackamas River. Oregon Highway 99E shield sign on the far right and Clackamas River sign. This steel arch bridge located on McLoughlin Blvd. was also known as the Dr. John McLoughlin Memorial Bridge, built in 1933 by Conde McCollough.

Highway 99E Milwaukee, Oregon late 1940's Main Street businesses. Four lanes, two-way traffic. Milwaukee had been referred to as the "Cradle of West Coast Fruit Industry."

The Bomber Gas Station—Milwaukee, Oregon

Oregon native Art Lacey, a former U. S. Army Engineer and aviation buff, was looking for a gimmick to attract customers to his gas station at 13513 S. E. McLoughlin Blvd. (99E) in Milwaukee, Oregon. So he did what most people would do … he purchased a B17 WW11 bomber for $13,750 and had his buddies fly it to Oregon from Oklahoma where he had it installed on top of his gas station.

This was no small feat. Once the plane arrived in Troutdale, near Portland, he needed permits to transport it to his location on McLoughlin Blvd. Once the plane was dismantled, it took four trucks and two lanes of highway to truck it twenty miles at 2:00 a.m. in the morning. The "Bomber Gas Station" was born in 1944. A drive-in restaurant was added in 1948. It was quite an attraction and business increased so much that forty pumps were in operation. Lacey soon claimed to be the "nation's largest independent service station." He also offered the public free bomber inspections with access to the plane's interior.

In the early 1990's seventy-five pumps were still operating, but business began to slow down as the old plane was showing signs of deterioration due to the climate and vandalism. In 1991 Lacey pulled the pumps and stopped selling gas because of new and restricting environmental laws.

Art Lacey died in 2000 at the age of 87. His plane was removed for preservation with the help of the B17 Alliance. Once restoration was completed, the plane was christened the "Lacey Lady." The gas station is gone, but the "Bomber Complex" still consists of a World War 11-themed restaurant and museum. The museum, housed in the old welding bay, contains WW11 memorabilia and a reference library.

The Bomber Gas Station, Highway 99E. Milwaukee, Oregon located at 13515 S. E. McLoughlin Blvd. A 1960's view.

Oregon Auto Camps

In the decade of the 1910's Oregon was a leader in auto travel because of its finely constructed roads for scenic travel. It was one of the first to establish a highway department requiring a gas tax and registration of drivers.

The Pacific Highway connecting California with Oregon made car travel possible, and Oregon pushed for new visitors and settlers to come; but the only accommodations were hotels or auto camps. Early camps were located on private property outside the city limits in an effort to evade lodging regulations. Realizing a need for lodging, local governments began operating municipal auto camps and charged a fee. These camps evolved into motor courts, and motor courts became the motels we know today.

COME TO NELSON'S CABINS FOR CLEAN, MODERN CABINS WITH GOOD BEDS AT MODERATE RATES, DOUBLES AND SINGLES. HWY. 99 E., 2 MI. SO. OF PORTLAND. PHONE 3-7511, P. O. BOX 93, MILWAUKIE, ORE.   C-526

Milwaukee, Oregon. "Come to Nelson's Cabins for clean, modern cabins with good beds at moderate rates; "doubles and singles. 99E, two miles South of Portland. This 1930's-40's view shows garages between the cabins and a dirt driveway. In 1948 Nelson's had fourteen cabins renting for $3.50 to $7.00 for a single and $5.00 to $8.00 for a double. Hot and cold running water, private toilets and baths, kitchens with utensils, and dishes. Cabins built in pairs with locked garages in-between.

Interstate Bridge aka Pacific Highway Bridge

Hailed as the "engineering marvel of the Northwest," the Interstate Bridge was completed in 1917 and took ten years to complete at a cost of $1,750,000. This ended the ferry service ran for many years between Portland and Vancouver. Also known as the Pacific Highway Bridge in 1917, it carried two-way traffic between Portland, Oregon and Vancouver, Washington. The vertical lift bridge spanning the Columbia River and measuring 3,548 feet long with a 38 foot wide deck, allows river traffic to pass under it. In 1958 a "twin" was built alongside the original bridge. In the 1960's the bridge carried two lanes of Northbound traffic on US 99, and motorists had to pay a 25 cent toll to cross. Portland, known as "The Rose City," is where US 99 branches into East and West for a hundred miles. The two highway 99's run down opposite sides of the Willamette River until they unite at Junction City.

Pacific Highway Interstate Bridge between Vancouver, Washington and Portland, Oregon, 1920's. "This bridge was erected in 1917 at a cost of $1,500,000 and was paid for by the counties of Clark of Washington and Multnomah of Oregon."

Pacific Highway Interstate Bridge has twenty-seven piers including approaches and fifteen spans with main channel; pre-1918.

Pacific Highway Interstate Bridge length includes approaches, four miles, marking it one of the longest steel bridges in the world. Cost $1,750,000; took two years to build, Vancouver, Washington-Portland, Oregon.

Pacific Highway Interstate Bridge crosses Columbia River between Portland and Vancouver; pre-1918.

Interstate Highway, Portland, Oregon/Vancouver, Washington. Waddle's Coffee Shop and Car Service. Snowy Mt. Hood in background. Drug Store next door. Waddle's was founded in 1938 by Gene and Natha Waddle and opened at this site in 1945. It closed in 2004 to make way for HOOTER'S restaurant.

Waddle's advertisement."We now have two modern drive-in coffee shops. No. 1 opposite Jantzen Beach Park on Highway 99 just south of Columbia River. No. 2 on 99E at S. E. Holgate, 4 miles South of downtown."

Portland Auto Camp

Located at 9000 N. Union Avenue on the Pacific Highway, the Portland Auto Camp claimed to be the "Best in Portland." It opened in 1925 on forty acres with forty duplex cottages and five hundred tent spaces shaded under cottonwood trees; later increased to seventy-five cottages. The camp offered folding beds, gas heaters, private toilets, and kitchens. There was a Community House with cozy fireplace and a radio and phonograph for listening pleasure. On the property was a laundry, bathhouse, and store that sold groceries, meats, and vegetables. In the 1930's the cabins became homes for long term residents, but a flood in 1948 wiped out the camp bringing the auto camp era to a close.

Portland Auto Camp located near Jantzen Beach, 75 modern cottages only 15 minutes from the heart of Portland. Shady grove for over 500 tent campers with every modern convenience. Cross any bridge to Union Avenue and turn left.

Portland Auto Camp Grounds. Entrance and Community House, 1920's.

Westside Auto Camp

It was the earliest camp in Southwest Portland with its beginnings in 1917. Dr. Edward A. Pierce bought the 1882 Slavin House which he remodeled. He added twenty-five cabins and opened it as the Pierce TB Sanitarium. It closed in 1925 and the land and buildings were leased to the Battey's who converted the Sanitarium into the Portland Westside Auto Camp. It got it's name from Westside Pacific Highway. In 1926 the Battey's demolished the Slavin house and used the wood to construct twenty-five additional cabins operating as an auto camp.

Located at the NE corner of SW Capitol Highway and SW Sunset, the auto camp ... over time ... converted into a motel and finally a trailer park. It was still in business as of 1952, but today the site is occupied by apartments, homes, and commercial buildings.

From the South: TAKE WEST SIDE PACIFIC HIGHWAY NO. 3 AT JUNCTION CITY, BY WAY OF CORVALLIS, McMINNVILLE AND NEWBERG. From North or East: CROSS ANY WILLAMETTE RIVER BRIDGE, DRIVE SOUTH ON SIXTH STREET OVER TERWILLIGER BOULEVARD TO AUTO CAMP.

Portland Westside Auto Camp. "From the south, take Westside Pacific Highway No. 3 at Junction City by way of Corvallis, McMinnville and Newberg. From the North or East, cross any Willamette River Bridge, drive south on Sixth Street over Terwilliger Blvd. to auto camp. 43 cottages, every modern convenience; showers, laundry, gas, water. On the left of real estate is beautiful grove for campers. Register at office."

Portland West Side Auto Camp brass skeleton key to cottage #16.

Message on back: "July 9, 1922. Our car and tent in auto camp at Portland, Oregon."
1922 California license plate. Exact auto camp not identified, but could have been the
Portland West Side Auto Camp.

The Colonial Village Motor Court, Portland; 6 miles South of City Center on Hwy
US 99W. Late 1930s-40s. Captioned: Barbur Blvd at SW 47th Ave. Twenty cottages
with garage, restaurant, excellent food.

TWIN CEDARS AUTO COURT — PORTLAND, OREGON

8911 BARBUR BLVD. (S. W. Pacific Highway 99W)

9A-H2586

Twin Cedars Auto Court, Portland 8911 Barbur Blvd (SW Pacific Hwy 99W). 17 modern cottages in various sizes—each equipped for comfort and convenience. Quiet and 7 minutes from City Center. Very comfortable beds, reasonable rates. Sender's message: "We are in first cabin beyond drive on right. The first place on right is the office and manager's house. It's quite a drop down to cabins from main highway. A nice place. AAA inspected. Pretty entrance from 99W." 1940's.

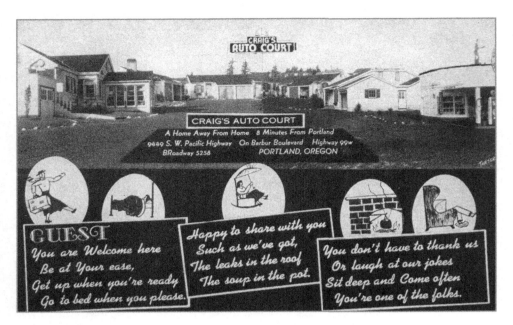

Craig Auto Court. 8 minutes from Portland. 9449 SW Pacific Hwy on Barbur Blvd. Gas pump visible on right. 1940's.

Stashe's Hollywood Motel. 10138 SW Barbur Blvd, 99W, Portland. 12 minutes to City Center. New, truly modern fireproof with solid tile bathroom and glass door showers. Hot water heat. Kitchenettes Separate accommodations for your pets. 1940's.

Englewood Motel, 10717 SW Pacific Hwy, US 99W, Portland. 1940's. Highway in foreground. Telephone booth at office building. AAA approved.

Cummings Motel in Portland. 52 units right in the city. "Enjoy cool, clean, quiet apartments. Tubs, showers, electric heat, kitchenettes, telephones, garage, city transportation at the door. Across from Overlook Park and playground. 24 hour nearby restaurant. Price $4.50 to $12.00 accommodate one guest or a part of six." 3620 N. Interstate. 1940's.

Paul Bunyan
Kenton District, Portland, Oregon

Paul Bunyan statue; Kenton District, Portland. Located at the corner of N. Interstate Avenue and Denver Avenue, the 30 foot Paul Bunyan statue is made of steel and concrete plaster. Placed on the National Register of Historic Places in 2009, it's the only statue in Oregon with that honor.

Paul was created in 1959 to mark the Oregon Centennial and was commissioned by the Kenton Businessman's Club as a way of greeting visitors. Paul was designed by the father and son team of Victor R. and Victor A. Nelson of the Kenton Machine Works and built using the skills of local welders, iron workers, and plasterers. Carrying a giant ax, he wears a red and white plaid lumberjacktype shirt and black boots; his full black beard showing off his big white teeth. After the Oregon Centennial celebration was over, the tourist information booth stayed at its location until 1964 when Interstate 5 was rerouted taking travelers away from the Kenton neighborhood. This led to the demise of the once busy district where Highway 99 used to go through the heart of Kenton. And such is the story of so many small town motels, restaurants, gas stations, and Main Street businesses that fell victim to the new Interstate 5 freeway. Of course, miles and miles of Old 99 still exist in California and Oregon, but it's no longer widely used as a main destination route.

OREGON

HIGHWAY MAP

Baldock Safety Rest Area, on Interstate 5

1968 Oregon Highway map showing an aerial view of Baldrock Rest Area now known as French Prairie, 14 miles South of Portland. Map courtesy of Oregon Department of Transportation.

Carole MacRobert Steele

BIBLIOGRAPHY

———∞∞∞———

Books

American Guide The Mountain States, The West Coast. New York, NY: Hastings House, 1949.

Apperson, Lee; Brooks, Donna; Park, Dorothy, *Sisson—Mt. Shasta The Early Years.* Centennial Edition, Mt. Shasta, CA: 1987.

Baeder, John, *Gas, Food, and Lodging.* New York, NY: Abbeville Press, 1982.

Baskas, Harriet, *Oregon Curiosities,* Guilford, CT: Insiders Guide, 2007.

Bogdan, Robert, Weseloh, Todd, *Real Photo Postcard Guide,* Syracuse, NY: Syracuse University Press, 2006.

Booth, Percy, *Grants Pass the Golden Years,* Coos Bay, OR: BandB Publishing, 1996

Bottenberg, Jeanna and Ray, *Vanishing Portland,* San Francisco, CA: Arcadia Publishing, 2008.

Brumfield, Kirby, Martin, Mary L., *Greetings From Portland,* Atglen, PA: Schiffer Publishing, 2007.

Brew, Jo, *Oregon's Main Street: U.S. Highway 99 The Stories,* Lorane, OR: Groundwaters Publishing, 2013.

California In the 1930's, *WPA Guide to the Golden State*, Berkeley, CA: University of California Press, 2013.

Carolan, Herbert, *Motor Tales and Travels In and Out of California,* New York, NY: G. P. Putnam's Sons, 1936.

Culp, Edwin D., *Oregon the Way It Was,* Caldwell, ID: Caxton Printers, Ltd., 1981.

Davis, Jeff, Eufrasio, Al, *Weird Oregon,* New York, NY: Sterling Publishing Co., 2010.

Drury, Wells, *California Tourist Guide and Handbook,* London, England, 2015.

Engeman, Richard H., *The Oregon Companion,* Portland, OR: Timber Press, 2009.

Fiorini-Jenner, Gail L., Tickner, Bernita L., *Postcards From the State of Jefferson,* Charleston, SC: Arcading Publishing, 2017.

Fiorini-Jenner, Gail L., Tickner, Bernita, *The State of Jefferson*, San Francisco, CA: Arcadia Publishing, 2005.

Fiorini-Jenner, Gail L, Tickner, Bernita L., *The State of Jefferson, Then and Now*, San Francisco, CA: Arcadia Publishing, 2007.

Flood, Chuck, *Oregon's Highway 99*, Charleston, SC: Arcadia Publishing, 2016.

Frank, Emilie A., *Mt. Shasta—California's Mystic Mountain*, Hilt, CA: Photofix Publishing, 1998.

Friedman, Ralph, *Oregon For the Curious*, Portland, OR: Pars Publishing Co., 1972.

Gribskov, Cheryl, *How to Thrive on I-5*, Salem, OR: Superlative Scribe Services, 1991.

Gulick, Bill, *Roadside History of Oregon*, Missoula, MT: Mountain Press Publishing Co., 1991.

Jakle, John A., Rogers, Jefferson S., Sculle, Keith A., *The Motel In America*, Baltimore, MD: Johns Hopkins University Press, 1996.

Livingston, Jill, *That Ribbon of Highway 1: Highway 99 from the Oregon Border to the State Capital*, Klamath River, CA: Living Gold Press, 2000.

Livingston, Jill, *That Ribbon of Highway 111: Highway 99 Through Pacific Northwest*, Klamath River, CA: Living Gold Press, 2003.

Momsen, Joan, *Journeys To the Past-The Roads Least Taken*, Grants Pass, OR: Josephine County Historical Society, 2013.

Margolies, John, *Home Away From Home-Motels In America*, Boston, MA: Bulfinch Press, 1995.

Margolies, John, *Pump and Circumstance-Glory Days of the Gas Station*, Boston, MA: Mars Bulfinch Press, 1993.

Newlon, Michael R., *U.S. Route 99*, Denver, CO: Outskirts Press, Inc., 2010.

O'Hara, Marjorie, *Southern Oregon Short Trips Into History*, Jacksonville, OR: Southern Oregon Historical Society, 1985.

Oregon Historical Quarterly, *Aspects of Southern Oregon History*, Portland, OR: 1995.

Pacific Coast Highways, *Automobile Club of Southern California*, Los Angeles, CA: 1981.

Provost, Stephen H., *Highway 99 The History of California's Main Street*, Fresno, CA: Craven Street Books, 2017.

Reminisce, *Family Road Trips*, Glendale, WI: RDA Enthusiast Brands, LLC, 2014.

Reminisce, *We Had Everything But Money*, Harlan, IA: Reminisce Books, 1992.

Russell, Tim, *Fill'er Up The Great American Gas Station*, New York, NY: Crestline, 2007.

Sund, Cheryl Martin, *Rogue River*, San Francisco, CA: Arcadia Publishing, 2009.

Sutton, Jack, *110 Years With Josephine-The History of Josephine County, Oregon 1856-1966*, Medford, OR: 1966.

Witzel, Michael Karl, *The American Motel*, Osceola, WI: MBI Publishing Co., 2000.

Wright, Jan, *Images of America—Talent, Oregon*, San Francisco, CA: Arcadia Publishing, 2009.

Youngblood, Dorothy, *The Open Road*, London, England: Chartwell Books, Inc., 2008.

Booklets and Pamphlets

American Trust Company. Colorful California Names. AMTRCO. 1954.

Automobile Club of Southern California. International Pacific Highways System. 1959.

Bywater, Sharon. Our Love Affair With the Automobile Begets Oregon's Interstate 5. Southern Oregon Historical Society Quarterly. 2019.

Callahan's Restaurant and Lodging. 1918.

Division of Highways of the Department of Public Works. State of California. California Highways and Public Works Official Journal. May 1938.

Drive Oregon U. S. 99. The International Highway. 1940's.

Fraser, Laura Kath. Weasku Inn—Oregon's Legendary Rogue River Resort. Vintage Publishing. 1998.

Josephine County Historical Society. The Old Timer. Vol. 34, No. 3. Journeys to the Past—The Roads Least Taken. 1999.

Olson, Gene. Southern Oregon Revealed. Windyridge Press. 1990.

Oregon Society Daughters of the American Revolution. Oregon Historic Landmarks Southern Oregon. 1974.

Oregon Vortex and House of Mystery. 2011.

Shell Oil Company Directory of Auto Courts, Hotels, Resorts, Oregon, Washington, British Columbia, Alberta. 1950.

Shell Oil Company. Shell Finger-Tip Tours U.S. 99. Oregon, Washington. 1949.

Shell Oil Company. Shell Resort Directory. Oregon, Washington, British Columbia. 1938.

Shrine Pear Bowl Game. Sixth Annual Souvenir Pictorial Booklet. 1951.

Sutton, Jack. Pictorial History of Southern Oregon and Northern California. GP Bulletin. 1959.

Wellsprings. Wellsprings Healing Community. 2018.

Newspapers and Articles

American City Magazine. "A Noteworthy Example of Stage Construction of Highway." May, 1930.

Asnicar, Tammy. "Jewel of Grants Pass is Getting Makeover." *Grants Pass Daily Courier.*

Bullard, Mary Ann. "Beautiful Bridges." *Grants Pass Daily Courier,* February 28, 2019.

Duewel, Jeff. "When Cavemen Roamed the Earth." *Grants Pass Daily Courier*, March 25, 2010

Duewel, Jeff. "Hugo History Tour on Earliest Motels." *Grants Pass Daily Courier*, May 31, 2010.

Duewel, Jeff. "Caveman Bridge Renovation Project To Begin Next Week." *Grants Pass Daily Courier*, September 3, 2017.

Duewel, Jeff. "Caveman Bridge Rehabilitation Getting Down to Details." *Grants Pass Daily Courier*, July 8, 2018.

Duewel, Jeff. "Local Icons Reborn." *Grants Pass Daily Courier*, May 1, 2019.

Duewel, Jeff. "Celebrating History." *Grants Pass Daily Courier*, May 5, 2019.

Hall, Shaun. "Traffic Through Downtown Dead with Opening of I-5." *Grants Pass Daily Courier*, March 25, 2010.

Hall, Shaun. "Climate Sign A Welcoming Message To Locals and Visitors." *Grants Pass Daily Courier*, January 27, 2011.

Hall, Shaun. "Old Friend Is Getting A New Face." *Grants Pass Daily Courier*, March 21, 2011.

Jetter, Roger. "One Small '49 Mercury and One Huge B-17." *Bangin' The Gears*, October, 2006.

LaLande, Jeff. "Lithia: Ashland's Famous Fizzy Water." *Southern Oregon Historical Society Newsletter*, Winter 2019-2020.

Momsen, Joan. "Signs of the Times." *Grants Pass Daily Courier*, November 4, 2018.

Momsen, Joan. "Signs of the Times." *Grants Pass Daily Courier*, November 18, 2018.

Momsen, Joan. "The Rogue River in Jackson and Josephine Counties." *The Silver Pages 2019.*

Morgan, Zoe. "Visitors Still Enjoy the Rustic Charm of the Weasku Inn." *Grants Pass Daily Courier*, February 28, 2019.

Nels, Jean. "History of the Mount Shasta Region." 2017.

Shinn, Troy. "City of Grants Pass Wants to Tear Down, Replace Redwood Empire Sign." *Grants Pass Daily Courier*, April 1, 2018.

Shinn, Troy. "Council Backs Teardown of Redwood Empire Sign." *Grants Pass Daily Courier*, June 19, 2018.

Shinn, Troy. "Council Says It Will Restore, Not Replace, Redwood Empire Sign." *Grants Pass Daily Courier*, June 20, 2018.

Shinn, Troy. "Advisory Committee Agree: Restore, Don't Replace Redwood Sign." *Grants Pass Daily Courier*, June 22, 2018.

Shinn, Troy. "Photos Show Few Alterations to Redwood Empire Sign Since It First Went Up in 1941." *Grants Pass Daily Courier*, July 8, 2018.

Stoddard, Scott. "Chorus of Voices Is Loud and Large—Save the Sign City Council." *Grants Pass Daily Courier*, June 20, 2018.

Stoddard, Scott. "Redwood Empire Sign Comes Down." *Grants Pass Daily Courier,* February 12, 2019.

Walker, Mike. "Historical Auto Camps and Service Stations—Hugo, Oregon Region, 1920's–1960's, Part I." *Grants Pass Daily Courier,* May 24, 2010.

Walker, Mike. "Historical Auto Camps and Service Stations—Hugo, Oregon Region, Part II." *Grants Pass Daily Courier,* May 31, 2010.

Whiting, Lisa. "Oregon Vortex, House of Mystery Draws A Crowd." *Southern Oregon Recreation,* May 25, 2017.

Maps

Automobile Club of Southern California. Outing Map Northwest Region of California.

Oregon State Highway Commission. Oregon Highway Map. 1968.

Oregon State Motor Association (AAA). Official Highway Map State of California. 1927.

Made in the USA
Middletown, DE
12 May 2022

65647311R00243